UA Training Technologies: 6

Design Skills in Human Resource Development

Design Skills in Human Resource Development

J. William Pfeiffer, Ph.D., J.D.
Arlette C. Ballew

University Associates, Inc.
8517 Production Avenue
San Diego, CA 92121

Table of Contents

Introduction

One of the most complex activities in which the HRD trainer or consultant can engage is designing learning experiences for client systems. Whether one is planning a course in problem-solving skills, a communications workshop, or a management-development seminar, several major elements and questions should be considered in designing training events based on experiential learning. In this book, we will begin by cataloging the major elements that must be specified and considered before designs can be built, the skills involved in designing adult-education events, components of designs, and considerations that must be taken into account in meeting the unique needs of the client system. Our primary emphasis is on integrating these considerations into an organic sequence of learning activities that are central to personal and professional growth and skill development.

It is realized to varying degrees within the training field that assessment of training needs, although it precedes design, is a different function from design. Similarly, evaluating a training program is different from designing or presenting the program. In many cases, there are good reasons why the person who determines what is needed is not the one who will present the training or the one who will evaluate its efficacy. There also are reasons—not always as good—why the person who presents a training program may not be the person who designed it. For example, a trainer may be hired as a consultant to present a training program to an organization. If the trainer is not also hired to do a needs assessment, either someone in the organization has done one or somebody (probably an administrator) has decided by some other means what the training should be about. In many large organizations, instructional technologists have responsibility for instructional design, and trainers present the programs. Public training events are generic in a sense; they are designed to fill a certain purpose, and it is assumed that potential participants will read the descriptions of the programs carefully and decide whether the training to be presented is appropriate for them—a sort of reverse needs assessment. Some training in organizations, particularly skills training, may be designed by skill experts and then turned over to the training staff. It also is not uncommon for the evaluation of training to be done by the person who asked for the training rather than by the training staff.

What this all leads to is that although the ideal sequence may be *needs assessment-design-training-evaluation*, and although it may be ideal for the HRD team to be involved sequentially in all four, this frequently does not happen. There are too many exceptions and variations for us to address all of them. Therefore, in this book we will discuss needs assessment and evaluation (as they relate to training design) as though they were part of a sequence of events.

A Background to Design in Human Resource Development

A Brief History of Human Resource Development

Prior to the late 1940s, group work was in the province of those in the "helping professions": psychiatrists, psychologists, counselors, nurses, and social workers. With the publication of Lewin's (1947) studies of behavior in small groups and the emergence of the National Training Laboratories and similar organizations, the field broadened considerably. The laboratory method of learning and change (Benne, Bradford, Gibb, & Lippitt, 1975; Bradford, Gibb, & Benne, 1964) furthered the concept of human relations training and the experiential approach. Participants in training groups (T-groups) identified problems that emerged, learned the concepts and skills required to deal with those issues, and collaborated in the problem-solving process. Training group leaders served not as instructors but as "facilitators." The group became more than a setting for therapy or an object for study; it became a vehicle for learning and change in a wide variety of settings. There was a shift from observers studying the group to the group members studying themselves. The term "helper" began to include all those who facilitated group work, including teachers, administrators, community leaders, change agents, and, more recently, managers and supervisors.

Group training usually takes place in a workshop setting. The primary focus is how the individual relates to and interacts with other individuals and with groups, in terms of such things as leadership and influence, handling conflict, expressing feelings, giving and receiving feedback, competition and cooperation, problem solving, and increasing awareness of oneself and one's impact on others.

In 1969, University Associates published the first *Handbook of Structured Experiences for Human Relations Training*; there are now ten volumes in all (Pfeiffer & Jones, 1969-1981; Pfeiffer, 1983-1985). Each of these books contains twenty-four structured experiences with guidelines for conducting the activity, processing the feelings and insights that emerge, and helping the participants to focus the learnings and plan applications in their back-home settings. The first *Annual Handbook for Group Facilitators* was published in 1972. In the 1973 *Annual*, the concept of the experiential learning cycle was refined, and University Associates became a primary proponent of the necessity of working through all phases of the cycle. There are now eighteen *Annuals*, each of which contains a variety of structured experiences, instruments, lecturettes, and articles designed to aid in the professional development of group facilitators. In the last two decades, we and other organizations such as NTL also have offered a variety of training programs for the development of HRD practitioners. The continuing popularity of these training programs and our HRD publications (as well as thousands of others published for training and development professionals, organizational consultants, and managers in the last twenty years) demonstrates that there is a real need for training and development materials and that they have become an established part of the way in which we live and work.

In the last ten years, the field has evolved considerably. Training and organization development have become recognized areas of professional endeavor. Most medium-sized and large organizations have recognized the need for training and development functions. Partly because of a misunderstanding of and reaction to the type of very personal experiences developed in early groups and in settings such as Esalen in the 1960s, and partly because of the realities of organizational life, the emphasis has swung away from purely personal awareness and toward the individual's impact on and contribution to the work group and the organization.

As training, organization development, and change agentry became part of organizational life, people began to realize the interrelationships among the various helping functions (personnel, training, organization development, and many aspects of management). A new awareness of what they were all about resulted in a new term and a "new" profession: human resource development or "HRD."

The field of HRD has grown extensively in the last decade. It has been estimated that organizations in the United States alone spend approximately $30 billion per year on formal employee-training programs. In addition, approximately $180 billion per year is spent on informal training and coaching (Carnevale, 1986).

Principles of Adult Learning

Fortunately, many of the key leaders in the field of HRD tend to be professionals in adult education, industrial/organizational psychology, or some other branch of the behavioral sciences. These people have a sound understanding of the principles of adult education, originally developed by Malcolm Knowles (1972, 1975, 1978). From their writings and examples, we have learned some basic truths about what we are trying to do. The foremost of these is that adults are different from children; they are aware of their abilities and their experiences and they *require* more involvement in the learning process. Others include the following (Goad, 1982; Hanson, 1981):

- Learning is a process—as opposed to a series of finite, unrelated steps—that lasts throughout the entire life span of most people.
- For optimum transfer of learning, the learner must be actively involved in the learning experience, not a passive recipient of information.
- Each learner must be responsible for his or her own learning.
- The learning process has an affective (emotional) as well as an intellectual component.
- Adults learn by doing; they want to be *involved.* One should never merely demonstrate how to do something if an adult learner actually can perform the task, even if coaching is required and it takes longer that way.
- Problems and examples must be realistic and *relevant to the learners.*

- Adults relate their learning to what they already know. It is wise to learn something about the backgrounds of the participants and to provide examples that they can understand in their own frames of reference.
- An informal environment works best. Trying to intimidate adults causes resentment and tension, and these inhibit learning.
- Variety stimulates. It is a good idea to try to appeal to all five of the learners' senses, in particular to those aspects identified by neurolinguistic programming: the visual, the kinesthetic, and the auditory. A change of pace and a variety of learning techniques help to mitigate boredom and fatigue.
- Learning flourishes in a win-win, nonjudgmental environment. The norms of the training setting (see Chapter 5) are violated by tests and grading procedures. Checking learning objectives is far more effective.
- The training facilitator is a change agent. The trainer's role is to present information or skills or to create an environment in which exploration can take place. The participants' role is to take what is offered and apply it in a way that is relevant and best for them. The trainer's responsibility is to facilitate. The participants' responsibility is to learn.

Traditional childhood learning, especially in public education, is oriented toward the teacher imparting knowledge to the students. Adult learning is a process of one person (the facilitator) providing the opportunity for another person (the participant) to acquire knowledge, skills, and/or awareness. Adults are more used to exercising choice; they demand more choice in the matter of what they will believe, make their own, and apply. For these reasons, experiential learning has many advantages over the traditional classroom approach, the primary one being that it is more effective—it works better. In fact, many educators now believe that it works better with children as well.

Readiness, Motivation, and Change

Individuals do not change unless they are both motivated to do so and ready to undergo the process. Adults come to training experiences with preconception about what will happen, based on their past experiences. Participants who have taken part in experiential education previously may feel relatively prepared to engage in training. For those who have not participated in this type of training, knowing that it will not be the same as the traditional classroom method may be a source of relief or one of anxiety and fear of the unknown. As we will discuss in more detail later, it is extremely important that the goals of the program be stated clearly and that the participants be advised during the first session of what they will be expected to do during the training program.

People who choose to attend a training program generally are motivated for some reason, but people who are *sent* may well not be. If participants have been sent to the training by their supervisors, they may be resistant. At the very beginning of the training program, the facilitator should define the objectives and state what the possible *benefits* of the training might be to the participants. Individuals' feelings of resistance need to be acknowledged and legitimized at this time. The acceptance and encouragement of the facilitator and the other group members can go a long way toward encouraging someone to at least "try it." If resistance is not dealt with, it can become a chronic problem for the group.

A primary factor in generating motivation is the participants' perception that the training is relevant to their needs. The enthusiastic recommendations of previous participants can help to create this perception, as can printed descriptions of the program that are distributed to potential participants prior to the actual training event. If an organization is sponsoring the program, it, too, can help to disseminate information about the personal and professional benefits of the training.

Once participants enter the program and questions of readiness and motivation have been dealt with and resolved, the participants will become involved in the process of change. This process, as described by Lewin (1947) consists of three major phases: unfreezing, change, and refreezing.

The Cycle of Change

Unless the participants have benefited from a considerable amount of previous training, they will come to the event in a "frozen" state in terms of openness to learning. Each will carry unexamined attitudes and habitual modes of perception and response. Before they can undergo change, they must unfreeze their typical attitudes and behaviors—a process that can be very threatening. In order to reduce the threat and the resulting resistance, the participants must examine their old attitudes and/or behaviors and decide that they are willing to experiment to see if some changes would be beneficial.

The atmosphere of the training group is important in facilitating change. The process is greatly enhanced when an atmosphere of support, mutual risk taking, and trust exists. The democracy and intimacy that are part of the group process support self-examination and reduce the risk of trying out new responses. In fact, the mutual process among participants creates a norm that makes change desirable, rather than a sign of weakness or failure. As participants become involved in the training group, they begin to share its responsibilities, and the group becomes more cohesive. Fears about changing are reduced, and risk taking is rewarded.

Depending on the training objectives, change can be facilitated by a number of techniques. Primarily it involves the participants examining some aspect of themselves or the area of focus, experimenting with new ways of thinking or behaving, learning new concepts that they can relate to their existing knowledge and use as models for new ways of thinking or behaving, and practicing the change with feedback and support from the facilitator and the other group members. Chapter 3 of this book will discuss the technologies that can be used to aid in this process.

Refreezing is the process by which the new attitudes and behaviors are integrated into the participants' own ways of thinking and being. This integration actually is not a frozen state, because the process of change is a cycle: once experienced it opens up the individual to experiment and change again. The extent to which this takes place depends on the extent to which the person *identifies with and internalizes* the change. This, in turn, is dependent on the degree and quality of support and reinforcement the person receives. If one's changed attitudes and behaviors lead to more satisfying and effective relationships or a greater sense of self-awareness, or if others provide positive feedback, there is an incentive to continue the change.

Experiential Education

Much of what is learned in HRD is generated by the activities and interactions of the participants in the learning group. Participants are encouraged to experiment with new ways of behaving. They abstract principles, hypotheses, and theories that have some action implications from their experiences. This process is facilitated by an experienced trainer or consultant who has a background in the behavioral sciences and experiential education.

The goals of a particular training event will depend on the needs of the participants. They may be learning how to listen, how to communicate better, how to work in groups, how to negotiate, how to solve problems, how to manage conflict, how to conduct meetings, how to conduct performance appraisals, how to plan, how to develop strategies, how to be a trainer, how to be a consultant, how to perform specific job skills, or any of numerous other objectives. The goals of experiential education, on the other hand, are more general. They are: (a) to develop physical, emotional, and intellectual awareness of oneself; (b) to learn how groups function and the consequences of different group actions or processes; (c) to learn how groups interact with one another when they are competing or cooperating; (d) to learn more effective ways to solve problems; and (e) to learn how to learn (Hanson, 1981). The latter is basic to all the other goals in that it is a process through which continued personal growth is possible. It requires a willingness to explore, to examine (including oneself and one's values), to experiment, and to take risks.

Experiential learning techniques are used frequently in conjunction with other approaches in order to balance the cognitive, physical, and emotional components of the learning process. For example, rather than just reading or hearing about decision-making processes, participants in a training program may be given a problem on which they must reach some agreement as a group. At the end of the time allotted for the group's work, the group members are helped to discuss and process their interactions in order to study how decisions were made and how these decisions affected the members' commitments to the final product. At this point cognitive material (e.g., theories or models of decision making) may be introduced. This cognitive material is better understood because the participants can link it to their own experiences and their feelings about the process. Later chapters in this book will discuss the various types of training technologies and tell how to link them to the goals of the training.

2

Pre-Design Concerns

Before a training event can be designed, the *training objectives* must be established. For training objectives to be clear, there often must be a training *needs assessment*. Also, it is much more difficult to design training if one does not know how and by whom the training will be *evaluated*. So, although needs assessment and evaluation are separate HRD functions from design, in reality they may be performed by the same people. Because of their interrelationships, they all will be considered to some degree in this publication.

Design is the bridge between *what* the trainer wants to accomplish with (or in) a training event and *how* it will be done. Before attempting to design a training event, one should have answers to eight basic questions:

1. *Why* is the training being conducted?
2. *What* is to be the focus of the training?
3. *Who* is to be trained?
4. *When* is the training to be done?
5. *Where* is the training to be conducted?
6. *Who* is to conduct the training?
7. *How* will the training be designed?
8. *Why, how, and by whom* will the training be evaluated?

Why?: The Needs Assessment

The preferred way to answer the "why" question is by conducting a needs assessment. It is one of the most basic skills in establishing objectives for a training event. Such an assessment can provide clarity about the expectations of the client system and can help to reconcile them with the needs of the participants (e.g., do you want skill training or awareness expansion, team building or communication training? What are the priorities? Can these be accomplished in time allowed?) There also can be several other beneficial outcomes, including the following (Warshauer, 1988):

- Increasing the commitment of management and potential participants to the training and development effort;
- Increasing the visibility of the training function;
- Clarifying crucial organizational issues;
- Providing for the best use of limited resources;
- Providing new program and design ideas; and
- Formulating strategies for how to proceed with the training efforts.

It is not always possible to do a formal or full-scale needs assessment (some clients are sure that they know what is needed and will insist that you do just that), but it almost always is preferable. As an absolute minimum, we encourage an informal needs assessment, i.e., obtain the answers (from at least a sample of the client population) to the following questions:

- Why is the training being conducted? What is the need?
- What is expected to change as a result of this training (e.g., knowledge, skills, or attitudes—for individuals, groups, or a system)?
- What will be the impact of this training (on individuals, groups, the system)?
- How will the learnings be reinforced?
- How will results be monitored/evaluated?

A number of techniques are available for obtaining answers to these and other pertinent questions. The facilitator must consider each method and determine which (or which combination) is most appropriate to the particular client system.

Data-Collection Techniques

Several methods can be used to collect data from the sources that are available. Some require the involvement of individuals or groups; others, such as observation and review of existing data, require less direct involvement. Frequently, two or more techniques will be used in concert (e.g., a survey questionnaire and interviews), thus expanding the range and type of information gathered. The following is a partial listing of techniques for collecting information. For a more complete discussion of data-collection techniques, refer to Bouchard (1976) and Nadler (1977).

Individually Oriented Methods	Interviews Instruments (Questionnaires, Surveys, etc.) Tests
Group-Oriented Methods	Sensing Interviews Committees Delphi Technique Nominal-Group Technique Brainstorming
Observation	Systematic Observation Complete Observation Participant Observation
Review of Existing Data	Sensitivity Originality

Individually Oriented Methods

Most data-collection techniques involve either the people who are to be trained or individuals who have frequent contact with them. These techniques include questionnaires, interviews, and tests. Each method has unique features that influence its appropriateness.

Interviews

The interview is one of the most commonly used methods for gathering data, but it is most appropriate when the following conditions exist:

- When the information to be shared is of a *personal or sensitive* nature;

- When some of the *questions* to be asked may need to be clarified or explained;
- When some of the interviewees' *answers* may need to be clarified or explained;
- When the data collector *does not know all the issues*, so cannot design an instrument that will pinpoint them;
- When the interviewer may want to *change gears or pursue topics further* during the questioning, based on the information that is received;
- When the group of people who will provide the information is *small* enough to allow one-on-one interviews;
- When there is *time* to conduct one-on-one interviews with all those who hold relevant information, as well as time to review the responses and extract relevant data;
- When the data collector has the *skill and means* to collate, tabulate, analyze, and interpret the various data that will be obtained.

It often is best if the person who will be conducting the interview is a neutral third party, i.e., one of the facilitators who will be designing the training, not the interviewee's boss or someone with an affiliation within the organization. This will increase the likelihood of an honest response and can help to eliminate any suspicion of bias. It must be remembered, however, that there are some people who will view any outsider as a "spy." It is helpful if the credentials of the interviewer and the reason why he or she was selected can be published in the system prior to the actual interviewing process. It is then up to the interviewer to establish a comfortable atmosphere once each interview has begun.

The following is a basic outline of a typical interviewing process:

1. *Starting Out.* One problem associated with data-gathering interviews is determining whom to interview. If a training program is to be conducted within an organization, it probably is a good idea to interview a cross-section of the prospective participants (and their managers, if the participants themselves are not all managers), as well as the person who has arranged for the training. Once you

have determined who will be interviewed, provide the people to be interviewed with enough notice of or details about the meeting for them to prepare themselves adequately. An unprepared interviewee usually can offer only opinions, unsubstantiated by "hard" data. Such information also may be superficial, especially if the interviewee is relatively unfamiliar with the subject or the interviewer is not highly skilled in interviewing techniques.

When selecting a room for the interview, pay attention to the surroundings. Seating should be comfortable but not too comfortable. The person being interviewed should not be faced with bright light from a window or other source. There should be a table or other writing surface for taking notes.

Plan the interview time so as to eliminate interruptions. This may mean scheduling it early or late. Be there a little early to organize your thoughts and materials, and start on time. If possible, know the name and position of the person to be interviewed and his or her relationship to the rest of the potential participant group. Welcome the person by name, offer a seat, and introduce yourself, stating why you are there. State the purpose of the interview, who else will be interviewed, and how the data will be used.

Next, describe the norms that you would like to establish, e.g., honesty and risk taking. Make it clear that what the interviewee says will be anonymous but not confidential; that is, the data from all interviews will be tabulated and reported, but "who" said "what" will not be revealed. Encourage the person to try to relax and to say what he or she really thinks or feels. Ask the person to agree to tell you if you do not ask questions clearly. Then explain the procedure: say that you will take notes (or record the answers) while the person is talking to be sure that you get the real meaning of what is said, rather than relying on your memory of it. Obtain written or recorded permission if you will be recording the person's responses on tape. Say that you will review your notes with the person at the end of the interview in order to check the phrasing. Finally, estimate the amount of time that the interview will take.

2. *Asking Questions.* Prepare the questions that you will ask ahead of time, so that when actually conducting the interviews you ask everyone the same basic questions. (Of course, during the course

of a particular interview, you can ask the individual additional questions to clarify an answer or to follow new, pertinent trains of thought.) Check to make sure that you understand the questions that you will be asking.

Put the questions in a logical sequence, starting with less complicated and less threatening questions first. Ask open-ended questions, such as "why...," "how...," "what...," and "what do you think about...?" This allows the person to explain facts, details, and reasons while answering the question. Do not phrase questions negatively because this could be seen as biased; make them neutral. For example, rather than saying "Don't you think that...," ask "How do you think...?" It is important not to bias the question or lead the witness into any particular type of response.

While the interviewee is talking, take notes, using the person's own words. Try to maintain an interested, encouraging appearance and—above all—do not criticize the person's answers, rationale, or phrasing. If it is necessary to ask questions of clarification, make it clear that you are doing so merely in order to be sure that you understand accurately what the person is trying to say. This is a good time to practice active listening. Watch for verbal and nonverbal cues that could indicate that the interviewee is reluctant to discuss a particular subject, uncomfortable with the interview, overly eager to press a certain point, confused, tired, etc. You may need to change your manner of questioning or take a different tack.

If unfavorable information is introduced, there always is the fear that the source of the information will be revealed. Unless an atmosphere of trust is developed with the interviewee, the information shared may be slanted. It can take time to develop a trusting relationship. Some people never will "open up" to an interviewer, and many people will tell only what they think the interviewer wants to hear. Information acquired under such circumstances should be evaluated carefully and compared with data acquired from other sources.

3. *Finishing Up.* As you approach the end of the interview, wind down the complexity of the questions. Ask the interviewee if there is anything important about the topic that you did not ask or anything else that the person wants to say. Be sure to leave enough time to summarize the person's comments so that he or she can

check your understanding. Finally, thank the person for participating and reiterate what the next steps will be (that the data will be tabulated, how it will be used and by whom, etc.). Leave enough time to complete your notes before the next interview is scheduled to begin.

Instruments

The questionnaire, survey, or rating scale is another commonly used method of collecting data. Any instrument should be checked for its ability to measure what is desired (validity) and the consistency, over time, of the ratings obtained (reliability). Items or questions on the instrument form should not be phrased so that the answers received are biased. Closed-ended questions limit the responses an individual can make. For example, if the choices on a questionnaire are limited to "team development," "communication training," and "performance appraisal," but the respondent actually thinks that the problem is a lack of organizational direction, it is unlikely that the respondent will write in "more organizational direction" even if a space is left for "other." Another way in which bias can be introduced is through leading questions, those that indicate to the respondents how they are expected to answer. For example, if asked whether assistance in improving leadership abilities would be useful, who would say no? This does not, however, mean that leadership training actually is a crucial need.

For a complete discussion of how to select, develop, and use instruments (including organizational surveys and instruments used for research), refer to *Using Instruments in Human Resource Development,* the second book in this UA Training Technologies series.

Tests

Tests also can be used to assess the skills, abilities, or perspectives of an individual for diagnostic purposes. Tests are probably the least used of the assessment techniques, and are used primarily by designers of training programs to determine how accomplished the participants are before starting the program. This avoids repeating information that is already known or assuming too much prior knowledge. One of the major disadvantages of tests is that they frequently are perceived as threatening; as a result, people become quite defensive about their scores. If it is necessary to use a test prior to a skill-training program, the purpose of the test should be stated explicitly.

Group-Oriented Methods

In contrast to individually oriented methods of data collection, group-oriented methods allow people to receive assistance from other group members to support their views. Such techniques also allow members to "piggyback" on the ideas of others, generating expanded information. However, they also can limit opinions that do not represent the majority viewpoint. This limitation can be an advantage or a disadvantage, depending on whether the researcher wants a variety of ideas or ideas common to the majority of group members. The most commonly used techniques for collecting data from groups are sensing interviews, focus groups, committees, the Delphi technique, the nominal-group technique, and brainstorming.

Sensing Interviews

Sensing interviews may be preferable to individual interviews in terms of time utilization and group support of ideas, but they do have potential weaknesses. First, as with most data-collection methods, respondents must feel that their answers will be used in the intended manner. Trust of the leader and the other group members is a prerequisite to an honest, open discussion. Second, people who were not invited to be members of the group may think that they were excluded deliberately; thus, they may feel threatened. An explanation of the purpose of the sensing interview should be made to alleviate the fears of such people.

Focus Groups

This technique is used widely in marketing. A group of customers, users, or consumers is identified (often based on certain characteristics) and brought together to provide feedback on products, services, etc. It is much like a customer survey, but the respondents are not selected randomly. One pitfall of this method is that people may not be totally honest in their answers, e.g., they may say that they travel to Europe frequently because they wish they did or want to be seen as sophisticated. Recent studies indicate that focus-group responses tend to be more reliable if the respondents are rewarded in some way (a nominal payment or gift), because they then feel a responsibility to respond honestly.

Committees

Committees may be ad hoc or permanent advisory groups whose purpose is to provide input and guidance in program design. Alternatively, functional committees can provide insight into particular problems. Often, committee members can see skill deficiencies, attitudinal barriers, or other factors that hinder performance. Because of their expertise, they also may be able to specify what would be most useful in overcoming particular problems.

The Delphi Technique

The Delphi technique (Bunning, 1979) is especially useful if it is necessary to obtain information from individuals in a variety of locations. Generally, the process starts with the selection of a panel of individuals who are knowledgeable about a particular area of concern. These individuals are requested to identify the major aspects of a specified issue. These issues are then integrated into a questionnaire that is sent back to the panel of experts, who are asked to indicate the extent of the problem. The responses are summarized and returned to the panel members with another questionnaire. This time the experts are asked to complete the questionnaire and to explain their rationale for deviating from the mean group response on each question. The process reveals both the group members' opinions and reasons for differences of opinion.

The Nominal-Group Technique

The nominal-group technique (Delbecq, Van de Ven, & Gustafson, 1975; Ford, 1975) is somewhat similar to the Delphi technique. The major difference between the two methods is that in the NGT, the panel members meet as a group to discuss the various issues. The individuals participating in an NGT activity are given a subject or theme and asked to write their thoughts about the topic on a sheet of paper. The next step is to proceed around the group, asking each member to share one thought or idea with the group, in turn. These ideas are recorded without discussion until all ideas are shared and recorded.

The major advantages of the NGT are that it ensures that every group member contributes to the generation of ideas and that multiple facets of ideas are surfaced. It also helps to gain commitment from the participants because they have had equal opportunities to contribute and to evaluate ideas.

Brainstorming

Brainstorming is similar to the NGT. In this approach, ideas are voiced as they occur and are recorded without discussion of their merit. This allows participants to build on other members' ideas. Quantity of ideas is the first concern in brainstorming. After numerous ideas are generated and no new ideas are forthcoming, the discussion turns to the feasibility of the ideas. The major advantage of this approach is that "piggybacking" of ideas can occur. The technique does not, however, assure that all members will participate.

Observation

A third group of techniques used to collect data (and to verify data collected by other methods) is observation (Bouchard, 1976). The techniques range from observing a sample of behavior to some form of "undercover" observation by a concealed observer. The advantage of observation is that behavior is more natural and people are not required to provide the information directly. They continue to function as they would normally. Ideally, this would decrease the intervention impact caused by the data-collection process. Still, observation is likely to have *some* impact on behavior. Subjects being observed may "perform" for the observer and thus bias the data.

Systematic Observation

Systematic observation techniques frequently require a sampling of the behavior in question. For example, interactions between certain people could be observed on a random basis. After a series of observations, a pattern would evolve, showing what problems typically were encountered. If the observation revealed particular sources of problems, it might be deemed worthwhile to design a program (e.g., training in communication, listening, problem solving, conflict management, negotiation, etc.) to deal with the sources of the problems.

Complete Observation

Complete observation occurs when the observer openly uses a videotape camera, film camera, audio recorder, or other such technique to record relevant behavior. This method can yield massive amounts of information. It also can require large expenditures of time and money.

This technique can be used within a training program to record participant behavior during an activity. The primary purpose of such a recording would be to allow the trainer to discuss relevant issues with the trainees without interrupting the dynamics of the original session. However, it also would allow the trainers to analyze the session later, in order to improve the design of the training program. This type of observation also can be useful in analyzing meetings and other group events prior to and after a training intervention.

Participant Observation

In a final method of observation, the observer is also a participant. This may require the researcher to actually interact in a task-related way with one or more members of the group in order to learn what is involved in doing the work. Participation gives the data collector added credibility as well as relevant examples.

In another version of participant observation, the observer *sur-*

reptitiously observes the group. Ideally, this method reduces the bias caused when the subjects realize that they are being observed. However, because the observer is intervening in the group's activities, his or her actions can bias the results. A potentially more serious issue is one of ethics and credibility. One must consider how people will respond to data gathered by such means and whether they would trust a leader or trainer who used such techniques to gather data. This method would be especially counterproductive if the program based on the data were to require openness and trust among the participants.

Review of Existing Data

A review of existing data is useful in gathering information because the information is collected after the action, so there is no danger of biasing the behavior. An example of this technique is a review of critical incidents or performance evaluations to determine employee strengths and weaknesses. It may be possible to trace a number of incidents to common causes and, thus, to identify potential problem areas.

Although a variety of data are available in most organizations, there do not seem to be well-established techniques for collecting such data. Information collected often is in the form of case studies, which may be used to demonstrate a point during a program, indicate needs for program development, or verify the results of information acquired through other means. The keys to the use of this data-collection technique seem to be *sensitivity* and *originality*. One must be very sensitive to the type, quality, and initial purpose of the information being reviewed. Creativity and originality in interpreting and analyzing the data can lead to new insights. Historical data also can be used to supplement and confirm data collected from other sources and by other means.

Data Analysis

After the sources of needed information are identified and the data are collected, it is necessary to analyze and interpret the data. The procedures that frequently are used include some form of gap analysis, scaling methods, weighting formulas, and consensus. These procedures can be used to analyze data collected by a variety of techniques, and more than one procedure can be used to analyze a group of data. These techniques are as follows.

Gap Analysis	
Scaling Methods:	Rating Scales Rankings Nominal-Group Technique
Weighting Formulas	
Consensus:	Voting Compromise

Gap Analysis

A fairly easy method of analyzing data is examining the gap between where the organization or group "is" on a particular issue and where it should be or where it would like to be. The differences between actual and desired states indicate potential areas for program development. For example, a difference between 50 percent turnover for a particular firm or group versus a 10 percent average turnover for the industry would signal a potential problem. Once such differences are identified, it is necessary to attach priorities to the gaps to guide program development.

Scaling Methods

Scaling methods such as measurements on a continuum or rankings can be used to establish the relative significance of issues. Typical scaling procedures include the following.

Rating Scales

Scales frequently are used to show the importance or magnitude of various issues to the person completing the scale. The most frequently used is the Likert scale, on which the respondent indicates agreement on a continuum ranging from "strongly agree" to "strongly disagree." Other frequently used measurements include ranges of importance or desirability.

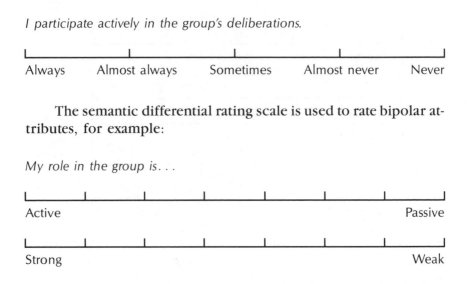

I participate actively in the group's deliberations.

| Always | Almost always | Sometimes | Almost never | Never |

The semantic differential rating scale is used to rate bipolar attributes, for example:

My role in the group is. . .

Active   Passive

Strong   Weak

A variation of this technique is to ask the respondent to mark a scale to indicate where the respondent, group, or organization is and where it should be on particular issues. This helps to identify major gaps between the current and desired states (i.e., training needs). Other types of rating scales include forced-choice scales and sociometric ratings (rankings).

Rankings

Various data can be rank ordered in terms of their importance, desirability, frequency, etc. Individual rankings then can be combined to establish the relative value that the group places on each issue. Sociometric ratings (of individuals) allow comparison (e.g., who rated whom or what lowest and highest), thereby generating more data than just the individual rankings themselves. The design and use of these scaling methods are described in more detail on pages 65 through 75 of *Using Instruments in Human Resource Development.*

The Nominal-Group Technique

In the nominal-group technique, discussed on pages 19-20, the participants in a group rank the items identified in the group discussion in order of importance. The responses of all participants are compiled, and the results are reported to the group. The group ranking then can be used to establish priorities for discussion, training, or other program design.

Weighting Formulas

One of the problems in using scales is that no mechanism is provided to indicate the relative differences in the importance of the scales. Weighting formulas allow the respondents or diagnostician to attach more value to one scale than another. A common weighting method is to ask the respondent to indicate how *important* a particular attribute (skill, attitude, need) is, how *frequently* the attribute is encountered, or how *deficient* the subject feels in terms of the attribute. In one example, a study (Thomas & Sireno, 1980) asked managers to indicate how important a particular competency was for their subordinates, how frequently the subordinates needed the competency, and how well prepared the subordinates were in that competency. These three responses were then combined to determine the need for a program to develop the competency. This study also identified substantially different priorities for job competencies among industries—again supporting the need to customize training programs rather than interpreting training needs to fit an existing program.

Consensus

One of the most commonly used methods of reaching agreement is consensus (a majority or all members agree on an issue, a ranking, or a next step). This is not to be confused with voting, compromising, or "horse trading." Although the latter often are easy methods for decision making, they may not include a careful weighing of all the relevant information.

Voting

If a group uses a nonquantitative method to collect information, a vote of the members often is used to determine the implications of the data collected. However, one or two persons or issues frequently dominate the discussion, or individuals with high status—such as experts or top managers—often voice their views on the subject. Unless there is information that clearly contradicts these high-powered views, the subsequent vote and recommended actions will likely follow along.

Compromise

If there are a number of strong feelings about an issue, a common solution is a compromise. This often results in a nonthreatening, suboptimum recommendation that is acceptable to all but will do little to solve the problem. In fact, a compromise program could worsen the problem by raising the expectations of participants. Then, if the expected results are not achieved, the program, its sponsor, its designers, and its facilitators look bad.

Summary

To design a training program or intervention, the program designer should consider the possible sources of data, how the data will be collected, and how the data will be analyzed. Although it is possible to build a program based on an interview with a supervisor or a few potential participants, a wider perspective is helpful in assessing the needs that the program should attempt to meet. In general, the more sources of information, techniques of data collection, and methods of data analysis that can be used to diagnose a problem, the better the understanding one has of the problem or training need.

What?: The Training Objectives

Once the needs assessment has been completed, the data can be analyzed in order to consider the focus of the proposed training and its aims or desired outcomes, *the specific ways in which people should change, develop, or behave.* With these in mind, the following points then should be considered; each will affect the training design (Cooper & Harrison, 1976):

Predetermined/Emergent Aims

* Who should determine the learning objectives (the facilitator, the participants, or both)?
* To what extent can learning aims be determined prior to the training experience?
* What is the possibility of additional aims emerging during the training event?
* To what extent might the facilitators impose, consciously or otherwise, some aims because of their own values and by setting norms?

Extent of Objectives

* To what extent are training aims conceptual (cognitive) or emotional (usually personal)? This will affect the nature of the design, the materials needed, and the type of facilitation required. (See more on this important point later in this chapter.)
* Are the training objectives remedial (focused on participants' weaknesses, problems, or lacks) or developmental (to build participants' strengths)? The extent to which activities are focused in either direction should be considered, as well as the implications of this focus.
* How long is the group learning intended to have an effect (days, months, years)? What reinforcement will be available to the participants to aid in the transition and refreezing processes?

Experimental/Experiential Aims

The choice between these aims has implications for the training design (e.g., the use of observers, data collection, process reviews) and for the facilitator's learning theory or models. Points to consider include:

- The extent to which the activity will be a joint learning experiment, in which the facilitator has a special responsibility (e.g., for helping the group to examine data in reviewing its work).
- The extent to which the facilitator allows participants to experience the activity without heavily processing it.

Identifying the Training Objective

To pinpoint the training objective, ask "What is expected to change as a result of this module?" In general, the training objective will fall into one of three broad categories:

- *Cognitive:* The acquisition of knowledge/understanding of concepts/memorization of content;
- *Psychomotor:* The practice and acquisition of new skills/new behaviors; and
- *Affective:* The development of awareness/exploration of attitudes/realization of preferences.

It is important to be clear about which of these areas will be the focus of the training. If participants are to be presented with a lecture on a particular topic, the training is in the cognitive realm (knowledge/concepts), and the objective would be to *tell* the participants about the topic or issue or to *acquaint them with its major points.* The objective is *not* to develop their skills in dealing with it (you cannot do that with a lecture) or to change their attitudes about it (ditto). Too often, training objectives are worded as "To change the participants' attitudes about. . ." when all that happens is a lecture on why they should or should not do something. (It would at least be more effective to state what would *happen* if they did or did not behave in a certain way.) Although the latter may bring about some change in peoples' behavior in certain situations (because of the understanding of the consequences), it is very unlikely to change their attitudes or opinions.

Knowledge and concepts can be communicated through training modules such as reading, lectures, and discussions. Psychomotor skills can only be imparted through "hands-on" (literally or figuratively) practice such as that provided by role playing, case studies, and simulations. Affective learning (e.g., awareness training or exploration and discovery of personal attitudes) requires the participation of the trainees. Their content—their thoughts, reactions, feelings, etc.—are a great deal of the focus of this type of training experience. Obtaining this information and working with it requires more facilitating skills than presenting skills. The training technologies that can be used in this realm are role plays, instruments, structured experiences, and intensive small groups.

Note that we stated the objective of this type of training as the awareness, discovery, or exploration of attitudes. Even with time to experience something and discuss it in a training group, participants are likely to need time to reflect (and perhaps to experience the effects of changed behaviors) before their attitudes actually change. As Leon Festinger's (1957, 1964) research in cognitive dissonance shows, if you can change the behavior, the attitudes are more likely to follow. It does not seem to work as well the other way around.

Wording It Realistically

The training objective should communicate the following:
1. What the facilitator intends to do, or
2. The expected outcome or benefit to the participant.

It is important in framing the training objective to be clear about what you will do and what you reasonably can expect to happen as a result of the training. It is folly to promise that training will "improve productivity in the organization" or "change the trainees' attitudes." One of these may be what you hope to achieve, but neither can be guaranteed or measured. Rule No. 1 is: do not promise more than you can deliver. This may require that the client be educated about the reality of training and the other factors that can affect the outcome of training. To be most realistic, a statement of training objectives would begin "It is expected that" (e.g., trainees will learn how to thread a needle as a result of this program). If this is not acceptable in one's particular situation, one still should resist making a statement such as "The trainee will be able to thread a needle as a result of the program." Training cannot control for other factors in the organization, the trainees' jobs and other environments, or the individuals themselves. All participants may not be able to attend all the training sessions because of other job pressures. People's skill levels are factors over which the trainer has no control. Also, although training can impact a person's comprehension and even ability, the trainer has little control over the person's *willingness* to use the new learning once the individual leaves the training setting. That, in fact, is the manager's responsibility. Too often, the people who are "ordering" the training expect trainers to assume this responsibility and to guarantee an unrealistic outcome. As Dr. Phyliss Cooke puts it, "You can swim in shark-infested waters, but you had better not leak any blood."

In writing training objectives, therefore, it is wise to stick to what you will do and what you expect to happen. Suggested alternatives are: "The trainer will demonstrate and explain how to thread and needle, and the trainees will practice this skill" or "The trainees will have the opportunity to learn how to thread a needle" or "The trainees will be presented with the theory of and practice in threading a needle." Other objectives can be "to explore," "to engage in," and so on. If the training is mandatory skills training, the objective can include an "or else" statement, e.g., "The trainees will learn how to thread a needle or they will not be certified (will have to retake the training, will have to be retested, etc.).

Other Major Design Considerations

Before the design itself can be considered, the other principal components of the learning environment—participants, group structure, physical concerns, and training staff—must be considered in relation to the learning objectives, and several questions must be answered concerning the specific learning experience being planned. One is not ready to design until one has answers to the who, when, where, and how questions.

Who?: Participant Considerations

The Number of Participants

It is important to be able to anticipate how many people will be involved in the training program because some design components require a large number of participants while others are designed to be used with very small groups. The size of the total group will dictate the size and number of small groups that can be formed to achieve various objectives. Subgroups of three to seven members each tend to be optimal.

The designer also must consider the level of affect (emotional response) that is likely to be generated by each design component. A facilitator can handle a larger group if there will be minimal risk taking, conflict, or emotional involvement. If participants will be "pushed," the facilitator will need to devote more time and energy to each participant, so the group must be smaller or there must be additional facilitators.

The Familiarity of Participants with One Another

This consideration is important in selecting learning experiences. For example, it may not be necessary to include "ice-breaker" activities if the participants are familiar with one another. What often happens is that some participants know one another but there is an unequal acquaintanceship within the group. The design of the training event should take into account that there might be some natural subdivision because of previous social acquaintance. One can capitalize on the relationships that participants bring to a training experience by using acquaintanceship as a means of support for planning back-home applications and for follow-through. However, although intact groups (groups with established relationships), such as work groups, might achieve a greater transfer of learning, the members also might be reluctant to be entirely open. Instead, participants who are strangers to one another (and unlikely to continue the relationship after the training event) may gain greater intimacy and openness at the possible expense of a less effective transfer of learning. It can be desirable to use this information in forming groups, assigning staff to the particular groups, and selecting activities for the beginning and end of the experience.

The homogeneity or heterogeneity of the group—the group composition—also needs to be considered. Heterogeneity can lead to greater confrontation but can provide the group with a wider range of resources. Homogeneity can lead to greater intimacy and affection among participants but also to less variety, which can restrict the learning possibilities available to the group. In general, heterogeneous groups are richer, but each individual needs to be able to identify with at least one other person in the group. It also is desirable if all the participants are at about the same *level* in terms of content background and previous training experience.

The Backgrounds and Previous Training Experience of the Participants

It is important to consider whether the training might be dissonant with the norms and culture of the institutional backgrounds of the various participants or of that within which the training is to take place. One might not want to ask the participants to learn and change their attitudes in ways that are contrary to the ideology of their back-home situations. The organizational climate of the client organization may not understand or be supportive of training, and the implications of this need to be considered.

Before attempting the design, the facilitators should try to learn something about the background of the participants in regard to experiential approaches to education. This includes information about the initial goals, needs, and readiness of the participants. It is important to know whether participants have been in similar training programs before, because they may already have experienced some training activities that are being considered in which the learning depends on the novelty of the experience to the participants. It may be that some participants have been engaged in activities that are highly similar to those that are being planned. This need not be a negative factor; people who have experienced similar training before may be formed into an advanced group; they may be spread out deliberately across several learning groups; or they may be asked to volunteer for demonstrations of here-and-now interaction.

In addition, it may be helpful to know what the attitudes of the participants are regarding one another and the stated content or objectives of the training program and whether they have received any preparation for the training event from the sponsor. The latter can be achieved by means of word-of-mouth communication, a memorandum to prospective participants, or a brochure that specifies the learning goals of the event.

When?: The Length and Timing of the Event

The length and timing of the training event are important in that the sequencing and timing of particular events are dependent in part on whether the training takes place at one time or is spaced over several meetings. Training that occurs weekly for an hour or two presents a significantly different design problem than does a one-day event. In many cases, a primary issue is how to accelerate learning within time constraints. In a brief contact design such as one evening or one-half day, some learning modules would not be attempted because either there would not be enough trust developed in the time available or more data might be generated than could be processed adequately. Likewise, spaced sessions (e.g., weekly two-hour sessions) probably would produce a less intimate and less person-centered experience, whereas more condensed or intensive sessions (e.g., a one-week retreat) might offer more personal growth. Spaced sessions may allow greater analysis of group dynamics and encourage members to "work through" issues between sessions.

Defined time limits within the event itself also can affect the training. Setting limits for various activities can encourage participants to express useful information by the end of the allotted time period, but also can establish the facilitator's role as the locus of control or authority. Similarly, the facilitators need to decide whether starting and ending times for sessions, break times, and meal times will be adhered to strictly or loosely. The facilitator should ask the person who is requesting the training program whether starting and ending times, lunch times, and break times can be arranged to suit the participants. If the client says "no," the time constraints are givens. Norms will develop as a result of the following factors: (a) the total time allocated to the group experience; (b) the time distribution (sessions at regular intervals, one intensive week, etc.); and (c) session time limits and adherence to limits.

Finally, if the event is to be conducted within an organization, the length and timing of each session should coincide as much as possible with organizational realities such as schedules, work loads, cafeteria hours, transportation, and so on.

Where?: The Location and Physical Facilities

This consideration is important in that it is easier to develop what is called a "cultural-island" effect in a retreat setting than it is in the everyday environment of the participants. It is more possible in a retreat setting to capitalize on the development of norms of meaningful openness, experimentation, and sensitivity in creating an environment in which people are genuinely resourceful to one another during the free time of the training event. Some of the most significant learning in HRD training takes place outside the formally planned sessions.

The physical facilities also are important; ordinarily movable furniture and privacy are desired. Auditoriums usually are too inflexible, and sometimes very large open spaces are detrimental to the training design. It also is important to anticipate whether the training event is likely to be interrupted by nonparticipants, telephone calls, and other annoyances.

The physical setup also can affect the training. The designers should consider where and how the groups will work; what kind of atmosphere the physical surroundings will create; and how the physical environment can be arranged to support the learning objectives. For example, different group arrangements can have different effects. A circle of chairs distributes power and promotes interaction. Flexible seating often is desired so that participants can move around, form groups, and so on. For processing, the fishbowl arrangement can be particularly effective. Tables can be a hindrance for attitude training, and sometimes even chairs can. In such cases, it is best to have circles of chairs or to have the participants sit on the floor. Wider tables create more distance and more formal interaction. People at the ends of rectangular tables tend to have more power and control. On the other hand, circular, square, and triangular seating arrangements tend to equalize power. No matter what the seating arrangements, it is best if participants select their own places.

Who?: Staffing Considerations

The sixth concern is the availability of qualified staff to facilitate the training program. This includes consideration of the personalities, styles, preferred learning models, philosophies, and assumptions of the various staff members, which might cause role conflicts. The following issues should be resolved prior to the training event, and the design should be agreed to by all who will be involved in facilitating the event.

Skills/Repertoire

The facilitators' ability to handle certain types of group experiences and their range of competence should be a major consideration. The design of the experience should take into account the capabilities of the staff members as well as their preparedness in attempting various learning goals. If the staff members are minimally qualified, it may be necessary to use a great deal of instrumentation and structure to make up for their lack of supervised experience. The intensity level of the training event also should be modified somewhat depending on the expertise of the available staff. If the credentials of the staff members are somewhat suspect, it may be necessary to develop fairly strict controls on the amount of affect that is generated in the experience itself; i.e., activities that might generate a great deal of feeling data might not be used because, in general, they require much more expertise on the part of the facilitators.

Personality and Style Variables

Some facilitators work more readily with their own aggression, some with their affection, and others remain detached and unemotional. These differences may be justified or institutionalized as differences in role perception and style, but they really may be attributable to personality differences (i.e., personal styles or social styles) among staff members. Because the models of role conflict and resolution of interpersonal differences in the staff team could influence the participants' learning, it is important to review style preferences when selecting the training staff.

Facilitators also may have differences of opinion about training approaches. The following are some examples of these and suggestions for handling them (Cooper & Harrison, 1976).

- *Mechanistic/Organic Approaches.* If one staff member insists on structuring a group experience, and another wants to respond to group needs spontaneously, the entire experience may suffer. In such a case, it is necessary to synthesize these two approaches into a productive design.

- *Modeling/Scanning.* Trainers who adopt a learning theory based on modeling might find that they are encouraging noticeable but short-term change. If, instead, they encourage group members to use one another as learning sources, through an approach based on scanning the interactions of group members, participants may actually show less change, but the approach may prompt major, internalized change.

- *Group or Personal Growth.* Staff disagreement about the level of intervention can create normative problems in that participants can receive conflicting messages about the learning objectives of the group. On the other hand, the conflict can provide the participants with a wider range of learning. These issues include the orientations of the facilitators toward (a) understanding the dynamics of the group or (b) developing the growth potential of individuals, as well as whether they believe that these orientations can co-exist.

Staff Composition

The composition of the training staff will influence the norms and learning objectives of the participants. The inclusion of both male and female staff members can provide opportunities to focus on issues that otherwise might not surface. Other variables include the number of staff members and the mix of staff members with different occupational identifications.

Administration of the Program

Finally, in planning the staffing of an event, it is important to know whether the trainers also will be the administrators of the program. This requires more time and effort on their part and may create a somewhat conflicting situation.

How?: Implementation Considerations

The Contract

This item may be the most important and it has two dimensions. First, it is critical that the facilitator have a clear sense of what the contract with the client system is. In the best circumstances, this consideration relates to one's skill in conducting a needs assessment, in determining learning objectives, and in specifying goals. At one end of the spectrum, the client may specify what is to be done (what type of training is to be delivered), although few clients have the expertise to stipulate how this is to be achieved. It then is the facilitator's job to determine whether he or she can accept such an assignment in good conscience. Generally, the client will ask for some type of training; the facilitator will ask relevant questions; and then the facilitator will suggest what type of training might be most appropriate, based on the completion of some degree of needs assessment. When the training to be delivered is agreed to, the means of delivery may be specified in the contract, or it may be left up to the facilitator to determine what will work. In such a case, the facilitator may want to leave some flexibility in the design in order to negotiate aspects of it with the participants.

The contract between the facilitator and the participants is the second dimension of contracting. It is important to narrow the expectation gap between oneself and the participants in the training event. It also is important to recognize that the psychological contract and the legal contract may not be the same. It is important that the goals and the learning method of the event be specified beforehand in language that both the staff members and the participants can understand. The design is far more likely to have a chance to be effective if the participants come to the learning experience knowing what to expect, why they are there, and what they have contracted to experience. However, it is also important to establish more specific expectations, behavioral norms, and so on, with the participants at the beginning of the training event. In some cases, this can best be achieved by means of a contract between the facilitator and the participants. Egan (1972) and Karp (1985) describe the development of such contracts.

Access to Materials and Other Aids

Access to training materials and other aids in terms of availability, budget, and convenience is an important consideration. Some materials, such as standardized measurement instruments, are expensive, and others require a great deal of time to prepare or assemble. Some teaching aids, such as videotape recorders, are difficult to carry from place to place. The facilitator needs to develop an inventory of materials that are available: newsprint flip charts, felt-tipped markers, easels, and masking tape; chalkboards, chalk, and erasers; blank paper and pencils; overhead projectors and other audiovisual aids; as well as work sheets, instruments, and handouts. It often is very useful to have duplicating equipment at the training site.

Opportunity for Follow-Through

A final consideration is the opportunity to follow through with the participants after the training experience is formally ended.

Although this concern is listed last, it is by no means of least importance. When developing a design for a learning event, it is important to know beforehand what is going to happen afterward. Is it going to be feasible for participants to meet again to work through the problems of transfer of training? Are they going to have access to one another on a day-to-day basis? Is the staff going to be accessible to them afterward? Is it possible to have follow-up sessions some weeks or months later to ensure transfer of training? Part of the application of learning to the participants' own work and social settings can be designed differently if there is an opportunity for some support and follow-through work after the training event is completed.

Prior to developing the design for a particular training event, the facilitator should explore what he or she has to work with in terms of time, space, staff, money, human resources, and materials. Once such an inventory is completed, the facilitator may conclude that the contracted goals of the learning experience are unattainable given the resources that are available. The facilitator then may want to renegotiate the contract or attempt to develop new resources for the event.

Why, What, How, and Who?: Training Evaluation

The issue of training evaluation raises several questions:

- Why is evaluation being done?
- What is being evaluated?
- Who should set the learning standards?
- Who will be conducting the evaluation, i.e., who will judge the results of the training (participants, facilitators, both of these, outside individuals or groups)?
- How is the evaluation to be done, i.e., how will results be monitored/evaluated? By what measures? By what criteria?

The answers to the first two questions will help to answer the overall question: "Should evaluation be done?" Evaluation is not always necessary, and unnecessary evaluation may not be a good idea because it is time consuming and expensive and because it generates expectations that something will be done with the data obtained. So the answer to the "should" question almost always is either "Yes, if. . . ." or "Not unless. . . ." Yes, if it is driven by a purpose: to *determine* something or to *justify* something. No, if the results will not be *used*, if the trainers or the client do not care what the results are, or if the subject matter or results may be too sensitive.

The purpose of evaluation is to obtain information. Before initiating or agreeing to an evaluation effort, it is wise to ask: What kind of information do you need? What kinds of questions are you trying to answer? What questions will give you that information?

The impetus to begin training and development in an organization often comes from management's belief that training is an important benefit to employees, that it is a worthwhile investment, and that it will help employees to fulfill their potential. However, management also hopes that it will increase personal and job satisfaction, increase motivation and productivity, and decrease turnover. In today's organizations, the emphasis often is on "the bottom line," return on investment. Managers and others who contract for training programs need to understand that it is impossible to measure the effects of training in such terms. One would have to measure *all the other factors* in the organization, over a stipulated period of time, in order to determine what part training played. Obviously, this would be almost impossible if not merely more time consuming and expensive than would be realistic. However, many managers still ask for training to be measured in terms of "increased productivity" or "effect on morale" or similar results. The HRD staff must educate such people in the realities of measurement and research. Behavior does not change in the moment at the time of training. A host of personal and organizational factors affect how well the training "takes" and whether changed attitudes or behaviors are permitted, supported, and reinforced in the work place. Too often, the people who expect an evaluation are as confused about what is to be measured as they are about why the evaluation is being done.

Probably the best reason for evaluating training is to help the facilitators to examine the design and to improve it, if necessary. Probably the worst reason is to prove that the training was worth the time and effort that it took. If those who are sponsoring the training (this problem occurs primarily in organizational contexts) do not understand the intangible effects of human resource development, the trainers would be wise to educate them or to seek work elsewhere.

What can be measured realistically is whether the participants were satisfied with the training; whether they felt valued because of having been offered the training; whether they thought it was interesting, helpful, or useful; and whether they think that they will use the skills, change their attitudes or behaviors, or have achieved some type of self-development as a result of the training. Some discrete skills also can be measured in a short period of time.

The most important thing in deciding to do evaluation is to be clear about why you are doing it, what or whom you are doing it for, and what or whom you are evaluating. Evaluation done for the purpose of justification is different from evalution done for the purpose of documentation, and that is quite different from evaluation done to determine something. The evaluation forms or survey materials should be geared toward obtaining the responses or the quantity and quality of information that you need. For example, justification might include the need to show that the trainees were satisfied with the training. The evaluation form then would not ask "Were you satisfied with the training?"; rather, it would contain questions such as "Which activity (or part of the training) was the most satisfying?" The report then could say that the data shows that _____ percent of the trainees found _____ portion of the training to be the most satisfying. For documentation, you may need to show that so many people attended, that there was follow-up, that the training was timely or what was requested, etc., or you may need to keep a head count in order to show that so many people were trained per year or that so many managers were included in the HRD efforts. In order to determine something, you need to frame the inquiry so as to elicit useful information (e.g., What other job skills would be useful in this training program? How do you plan to use this training?) The techniques used to obtain information for evaluation purposes are basically the same as those used to obtain information for the needs assessment (presented earlier in this chapter).

If the training facilitators are not to be involved in the evaluation phase, they should be permitted to assess the evaluation methods and to know who the evaluators will be. This is necessary for two reasons. The first is that one cannot design effectively until one knows what will be evaluated. When the goals of the training and the outcomes to be measured are specified clearly *and are related to each other,* the training staff has a clear notion of what to design for.

The second reason to ask questions about evaluation before beginning are related to professional ethics if not self-preservation. If it is not clear that the evaluation has a realistic purpose, that the proper issues or people are being assessed, that the methodology suits the purpose, and that the evaluators are qualified to conduct the inquiry, then the facilitators may well question whether they want to accept a training assignment that will be evaluated inappropriately.

3

Design Components:
The Training Technologies
and Other Activities

As we stated in the preceding chapter, the training objective, not the content area, indicates the design components/training technologies to be used in any training module and in the overall training design. Designing training for human resource development involves *putting together sequences of learning experiences— training modules—in relation to the goals of the event.* There are numerous ways to structure learning experiences; twelve design components are described in this section. In many experiential training events, some combination of these is employed to develop an overall training design. However, any one of these components or technologies may not be appropriate in all situations. One needs to select the technologies to be used based on the type of learning to be achieved (cognitive knowledge/concepts, psychomotor or behavioral skills, or affective awareness/attitudes) and the focus or content of the training.

The Involvement Continuum

The following[1] illustrates the relationship between learner involvement and the source of the content in training.

---

[1]Based in part on J. Hall., 1971, *The Awareness Model: A Rationale of Learning and Its Application to Individual and Organizational Practices,* Conroe, TX: Teleometrics; and R. Tannenbaum & W.H. Schmidt, May-June, 1973, "How To Choose a Leadership Pattern," *Harvard Business Review, pp. 162-164, 166-168.*

Involvement Continuum for Various Training Technologies

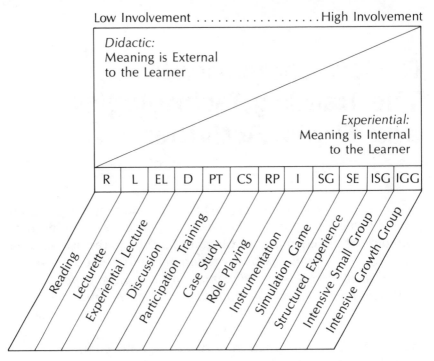

Low Involvement . . . . High Involvement

Didactic:
Meaning is External
to the Learner

Experiential:
Meaning is Internal
to the Learner

| R | L | EL | D | PT | CS | RP | I | SG | SE | ISG | IGG |

Reading
Lecturette
Experiential Lecture
Discussion
Participation Training
Case Study
Role Playing
Instrumentation
Simulation Game
Structured Experience
Intensive Small Group
Intensive Growth Group

Reading along the bottom of the chart, we see a classification of training design components, ordered according to the extent to which they incorporate participant involvement and the participants' content. The components on the left involve high *external* (facilitator-generated) content, low feedback, and high control of learner responses. These are the didactic techniques, in which meaning is external to the learner. Those on the right involve low external content (most of the content being generated by the participants' experiences, reactions, and insights), a high degree of feedback, and low control of learner responses. These are the experiential techniques, in which meaning is internal to the learner. Although the continuum in the figure has been described in terms of increasing participant involvement, it also can be viewed in the same relationship to other dimensions such as risk taking, self-disclosure, and interaction.

The least involving intervention is reading, in which the

learners are in a *reactive* mode, passively receiving and vicariously experiencing. The most involving interaction is the intensive growth group, in which the learners are encouraged to be *proactive,* to take responsibility for their own learning. In between these two extremes are activities that range from lectures to structured experiences.

It is our bias that the more experiential the learning can be, the more it will "stick." One cannot assume that complex material can be learned by listening alone (especially if that material relates to behavior). In fact, many studies (Knowles, 1972, 1975, 1978; Tough, 1979) have shown that adults learn primarily by doing. Therefore, our view is the goal of training should not be to teach a point of view; although it may be *understood,* it still remains the point of view of the teacher. The goal of training is to open up the learners to the exploration and examination of new concepts and new behaviors that they will choose to make part of themselves.

However, to accomplish one's training objectives, one must achieve the *integration* of both affective and cognitive learning (or affective, cognitive, and psychomotor in the case of physical skills training). Cognitive input, often in the form of models and theories, helps the learners to make sense of what they are experiencing and feeling. It provides a way of interpreting their current experiences and establishes guidelines for future behavior. It is especially useful in the generalizing phase of the experiential learning cycle (see Chapter 5). The infusion of cognitive material into the training experience (e.g., for knowledge/concepts training or to augment experiential learning) can be accomplished in several ways. One may provide a reading book or printed handouts prior to the training experience; one may provide handouts during the experience itself; one may deliver brief lectures (lecturettes) in large-group sessions, commonly called "community" sessions; or one may comment very quickly within an intensive small-group session about the theoretical implications of a particular set of behavioral data.

Readings and Handouts

There are two important things to remember in using printed materials in training. The first—and perhaps most often overlooked—is that they should be *readable* (clearly printed and reproduced). There is a better than average chance that bad copies simply will not be read. Working to learn is one thing; struggling just to read something is another.

The second dictum is that the readings must be *related to the goals and content of the training.* If a handout is on the same topic as the training but does not make the same points, it might confuse the participants or cause them to question the validity of the points raised. Printed materials should explain, supplement, or reinforce what is learned in the training. If a handout is merely for the purpose of acquainting the participants with other points of view that are not part of the training program, it should be distributed at the end of the session and its purpose should be clarified.

Lecturettes

A lecturette can be used prior to or following a learning experience to provide a kind of cognitive map for the experience that is about to ensue or it can be used to help focus the data from a particular activity or experience. It provides a way of helping participants to "make sense of" the learning that they are experiencing. It also can help to heighten the probability that the participants will relearn how to learn from their everyday experiences by providing them with a cognitive model for guiding their behavior.

The facilitator needs to develop a repertoire of lecturettes that can be used to highlight particular processes at any given time during a training event. The lecturettes in the University Associates *Annual* series and the University Associates *Theory and Models Kit* (Pfeiffer, 1989) are intended to provide resources for such brief, theoretical inputs. Because lecturettes frequently are used to augment structured experiences, many also will be found attached to specific structured experiences in both the *Annuals* and the *Handbooks.* More detailed information on the use of lecturettes can be found in the third of these UA Training Technologies books, *Using Lecturettes, Theory, and Models in Human Resource Development.*

Lecturettes are aided considerably by visual presentations. Sometimes the use of a flip chart can make a lecturette easier to follow, and the outline of the lecturette can be posted for participants to refer to throughout the experience. For example, a lecturette on the criteria of effective feedback can result in a poster listing such criteria. During the training event, participants can be guided in giving and receiving feedback by the set of considerations that become internalized through the experience. Sometimes the posting of such material serves as a means of guiding participants' behavior without the need for staff members to remind them of particular learnings. The seventh book in this set, *Presentation and Evaluation Skills in Human Resource Development,* contains more detailed information on the use of a variety of audiovisual aids.

Experiential Lectures

The experiential lecture is more involving than the traditional lecture because it incorporates activities on the part of the audience. Interspersed among the sections of content are brief inputs from or interactions among the participants, which fill out the conceptual input supplied by the facilitator. These interruptions are designed either to personalize the points of the lecture and/or to generate readiness for the next topic. (See Chapters 2 and 3 in *Using Lecturettes, Theory, and Models in Human Resource Development*—the third book in this Training Technologies set—for more detail on making lectures experiential.)

Discussion

Discussion is a time-honored teaching intervention that has been extended and refined in experiential training. It can be used in knowledge/content training to raise, clarify, or reinforce concepts. It can be used in skills training to exchange ideas and insights about how something works or to raise and answer questions. It is an essential part of the experiential learning cycle in awareness/attitudes training (see the discussion of the experiential learning cycle in Chapter 1 of *Using Structured Experiences in Human Resource Development* and in Chapter 5 of this book). It is, therefore, a component of the processing of all the technologies to the right of it on the continuum: participation training, case studies, role playing, instrumentation, simulation gaming, structured experiences, and intensive growth groups. In initiating a discussion, the facilitator is asking the participants to *use* the content of the training. They can be asked to use the points of the discussion to develop a list or to identify something to be used in the next activity. Facilitating productive discussion is one of the HRD professional's most valuable skills.

Participation Training

This includes training in participative skills such as listening, running a meeting, agenda setting, customer service, and so on. It is a type of "how to" or skills training. For example, if the training were designed to improve the participants' group-membership skills, the content might include cognitive input (lecturettes, handouts, discussions) on role functions in groups, group development, etc., and some activities to allow involvement and practice (e.g., role plays, instruments, practice, and feedback). It is toward the left center of the continuum because the emphasis still is on imparting information to the participants, although some of their reactions and experiences are included in the content, and they are provided an opportunity to practice and improve their skills. Skill development may be the most difficult type of training for the facilitator because it requires careful balancing and sequencing of both cognitive and participative design elements.

Case Studies

Studying a case scenario, analyzing it, deciding what should be done, and discussing it within small groups in order to make recommendations are more involving for the participants than any of the preceding technologies. However, case studies draw on less of the participants' own content than role plays, instruments, structured experiences, or intensive growth groups. The purpose of using a case study is to enhance the participants' abilities to think, to analyze (to use information), and to decide on a course of action. This provides the participants with an opportunity to explore their own thinking and decision making with those of others. It falls squarely into the realm of skill development, having conceptual components as well as experiential ones. Case studies can be used in a variety of settings; they most often are used in management, business, law, medical, and social-service training.

For guidelines on selecting, using, and developing case studies, refer to the fifth book in this series, *Using Case Studies, Simulations, and Games in Human Resource Development.*

Role Plays

In a typical role-play activity, a predetermined situation is acted out by the participants, but they provide their own words and methods of dealing with others. Reactions and results are discussed by the role players and observers, and then the same role players or new participants act out the scene again, attempting to apply the insights gained from the group discussion, focused toward a particular objective. Role playing generates a sample of each role player's own behavior, which is influenced by their feelings and responses to others. This affective (feeling) data becomes important content in the training; participants discuss their feelings, exchange feedback, and learn from the consequences of their behavior. Thus, with role plays we begin to tap into more of the partipants' content. We still may have the objective to expand some conceptual understanding and/or skill (focusing on whether they did it effectively) or generating awareness (focusing on how it felt)—maybe all of them in that order. Although role plays are extremely useful in helping participants to examine, practice, and develop skills in communication, problem solving, conflict management, and so on, they also explore the participants' feelings, responses, and insights about their own behavior and that of others.

In developmental role playing—in which the participants develop the problem or situation to be explored as well as the role-play scenario—the activity becomes even more experiential. The use of both structured and developmental role plays is discussed more thoroughly in the fourth book in this Training Technologies set, *Using Role Plays in Human Resource Development.*

Instrumentation

Instruments are questionnaires, rating scales, surveys, or other types of forms on which participants report information about themselves (self-assessments, styles, preferences, etc.) or their situations (families, groups, jobs, managers, organizations, etc.). The information obtained is *provided by* the participants (because it is their content, they cannot readily deny it) and is intended to be *used by* the participants (instruments are not tests). However, the focus or content of the information is based on a particular theory or model (e.g., styles of management, how people do something) on which the items of the scale or questionnaire are based. The participants' responses to the instruments are scored, interpreted, and discussed in terms of the theory or model. This is the didactic component of instrumentation.

Such nonclinical measurement or feedback devices can be highly useful in an experiential design. They can focus particular behavioral science concepts and can provide a set of data that participants can use in studying themselves intra- and interpersonally, in studying group composition, and in discovering new behaviors that they can practice within the relative safety of the training milieu. Instruments are not substitutes for experiential approaches but often can serve as highly effective means of *focusing* learning around a theoretical model. They are not to be used simply to present concepts because they invite the participants to explore their beliefs, reactions, and what they might do about them in regard to the subject matter.

In administering an instrument, facilitators generally will introduce it by encouraging the participants to be very open in responding to the items, then direct them to complete the scale or inventory, then deliver a brief lecture on the rationale underlying the instrument (the theory or constructs). They will then check understanding by having the participants predict their scores. The instruments are then scored (usually by the participants themselves), and the facilitators illustrate the interpretation of the scoring by using their own scores as examples. They then have the participants practice interpreting one another's scores (usually in helping pairs), with reactions following interpretation. This is followed by posting the data to build norms for the total group and then processing the data in intensive small-group meetings that focus on the personal relevance of the data at a relatively higher level of support than characterizes individual interpretation.

There are many sources of instruments that are designed to be used in human resource development. The Instrumentation sections of the University Associates' *Annuals* provide easy access to instruments that can be incorporated into a variety of training designs, and many of the structured experiences in the *Annuals* and the *Handbooks* also include specific instruments in their designs. *The University Associates Instrumentation Kit* contains 105 reproducible instruments from the *Annuals*, the *Handbooks,* and many other UA publications. UA and many other publishers in the field also offer instrument packages on a variety of topics. The second book in this Training Technologies set, *Using Instruments in Human Resource Development,* provides a step-by-step description of the seven phases in administering an instrument as well as guidelines for evaluating, selecting, and designing instruments.

Simulation Games

A simulation game is based on a model of how some system (communication, financial, organizational, etc.) operates. The participants assume roles within the system and manipulate the system toward some objective. In this way, they are able to discover the processes and interactions involved, be they human, financial, organizational, technical, or mechanical. As with most games, simulation games have rules of operation, and there are prescribed consequences for various moves. Learning is obtained through several means: working with others, working within the system, realizing the consequences of decisions/moves, retrying, and discussion. The participants are highly involved in the operation of the game, but the content is predetermined; it does not originate from the participants except in terms of their reactions, their questions, their learnings, etc.

Explicit information about the selection, development, and use of simulation games is found in the fifth Training Technologies book, *Using Case Studies, Simulations, and Games in Human Resource Development.*

Structured Experiences

A structured experience is a design module in which the participants learn through completing the experiential learning cycle (described in Chapter 5.) They engage in some activity that is designed to produce certain effects or learnings, they announce their reactions, they discuss what happened and what that means, they draw conclusions and make generalizations about their learnings in terms of the real world, and they plan applications. The structured experience is the only training technology that attempts to complete the experiential learning cycle in a stated amount of time. Thus, structured experiences stress high participation and processing of the data generated during interactive activities. Much of the learning content is generated by the participants; they reveal information to themselves about the topic or focus of the learning. Because the topic is narrowed and focused, it is relatively safe to explore it within the confines of the structured experience. The task of the facilitator is to take what is generated and, using the phases of the experiential learning cycle, focus it back down to the training objective.

A wide array of activities is available to the group facilitator in planning a structured-experience design. (For example, the University Associates *Annual* series, 1972-1989, and the *Handbooks of Structured Experiences for Human Relations Training,* Volumes I through X, 1969-1985.) The UA *Structured Experience Kit* contains all the reproducible structured experiences from the *Annuals,* the *Handbooks,* and twenty-four other UA publications. See also the References and Bibliography at the end of this book and at the ends of the other books in this Training Technologies set.

This technology is highly useful and flexible. Once facilitators have mastered the techniques of running and processing structured experiences through the experiential cycle, they can use them anywhere in which they fit. Any given activity may be appropriate in, for example, a leadership-development design or in one that focuses on team development, but because the goals of the two events may be significantly different, the processing of the data generated by the structured experience would be decidedly different. For example, there are several structured experiences in which small groups receive materials and organize themselves to construct something. In some basic types of training, the behavioral and feeling data that are generated by the experience would be processed in a group session in which people would focus on their own emerging awareness and on their feelings and reactions to the behavior of others. They would exchange feedback of a very personal nature about the effects of the process and the effects of one another's behavior. In a leadership-development or management-development workshop, the same activity might be processed in terms of leadership styles that emerged during the activity, styles of influence, roles people played, and decision-making procedures. There also might be an attempt to process the data in terms of a theory of leadership.

Structured experiences generate and focus data toward particular learnings, but the major skill in using them is in adapting them to the particular learning needs of the participants and in assisting the participants in processing and integrating the data that are generated. The first book in this Training Technologies collection, *Using Structured Experiences in Human Resource Development,* is a concise guide to evaluating, selecting, presenting, and designing structured experiences.

Intensive Small Groups and Intensive Growth Groups

An almost endless variety of small groups has been developed in the training field. At first, they consisted of the T-group or training group (see Jones, 1972), the D-group, or developmental group (which uses a variety of questionnaires, rating scales, and other instruments and learning devices in the place of a facilitator), encounter groups, counseling groups, and therapy groups. In all these, the participants engage in self-assessment, feedback, disclosure, risk taking, experimentation, and consensual validation.

All these groups are characterized by high participant involvement and interaction. The data for learning come from the life experiences and here-and-now reactions of the group members. Participants are expected to integrate their learning into new self-concepts on their own terms.

The use of intensive small groups is the dominant feature of experiential education. Perhaps the most well-known is the small discussion or processing group typically used in training and development work; this becomes the basic building block in the training design. A variety of small groups can be put together on a short-term basis for the purpose of processing the data of a particular learning experience, providing the opportunity for risk taking, trying of new behavior, or testing of ideas for back-home application. In addition, it sometimes is desirable to build leaderless activities into training events.

Ordinarily one wants to build as much heterogeneity as possible into small-group composition, with the stipulation that there be enough commonality among participants so that any given participant can identify with at least one other person in the group. It is important to establish some home base within the learning experience—a place in which participants can experience support and safety and where they can attempt to integrate what they are learning about themselves. The intensive, small-group experience becomes such a base.

Selection Criteria

Facilitators continually are faced with the task of planning activities to meet the learning needs of participants. The problem of choice can be represented graphically as follows:

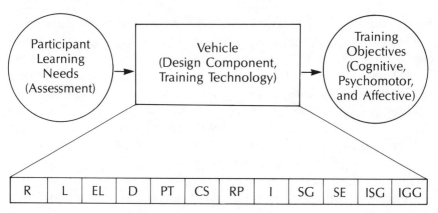

Each design component or training technology is useful for a different purpose, and there are training situations in which each would be appropriate. Thus, a design component, technology, or intervention is chosen after an assessment of the learning needs of the participants and a statement of training objectives and the type of training required for the particular module, at that particular point in the learning sequence. The time available, group size, nature of learners, complexity of content, possible resistance, materials, staff, and physical arrangements also are considerations.

In training modules that are focused on cognitive learning— the understanding of concepts and the assimilation of knowledge— readings and handouts, lecturettes, experiential lecturettes, and discussion are used primarily. In skills training, the design components on the left of the continuum may be used to establish a background, and case studies, simulation games, and role plays may be added to provide the simulation of actual experience and to allow the participants to practice, receive feedback on their actions, and retry. With the experiential approaches found on the right half of the continuum—those that primarily stress active participant involvement versus passive receptivity—the learning is more affective and presumably is internalized more effectively. To provide highly experiential learning, role plays, instruments, structured experiences, and intensive small groups can be used in combination with lecturettes, handouts, discussions, etc., in an almost infinite variety of highly innovative, flexible designs.

The maturity of the group, the skill and experience of the facilitator, and the environment in which the training takes place also help to determine which approach is used.

In the next chapter, we will discuss some major considerations within the training design to ensure that these components are utilized effectively.

4

Design Skills

Identifying Goals/Objectives

The ability to develop a learning design that is relevant and effective is dependent on a number of skills on the part of the small-group facilitator. The major set of skills relates to the ability to identify the learning goals of the training event very specifically. Two elements are important here: the first is determining whether the training that has been requested is appropriate to the people who will be attending. If the goals of the event are not appropriate to the participant group, they may well have a negative reaction to the training, ranging from confusion to resistance and resentment.

The second element is being clear about what the real goals of the training are and how they will be achieved. It cannot be stressed enough that experiential education is goal oriented, and it is important for the facilitator to learn ways to be able to clarify the goals for a particular training event *or a particular part* of a training event so that they are the drivers of and motivators for the particular learning experience itself. The two mistakes most often made in this area are misrepresenting what will be accomplished during the event and using design components ineffectively.

A classic example of the first error is stating that the participants' attitudes will be changed or that they will learn new skills and then designing a program to disseminate information. Training modules that consist primarily of content that the facilitator wants to impart to the trainees fall into the *cognitive* area, which we will refer to hereafter as *knowledge/concepts* or "K". These include learning and using rules, classifying and recognizing patterns, identifying symbols, detecting, making decisions, and recalling bodies of knowledge. The design components through which this is achieved are found on the left side of the involvement continuum; they include readings and handouts, lectures, and discussions. These require the trainer to have good presentation skills.

Training that is designed to improve the participants' *skills* must go beyond didactic components and allow for practice, feedback, processing discussions, and more practice. This includes performing gross motor skills, steering and guiding-continuous movement, positioning movement and recalling procedures, and verbal communication. Models and procedures become an important part of the content. Some of the trainees' reactions and insights also become part of the learning content in this area. Because skill training in HRD often involves verbal and behavioral skills as well as psychomotor skills, we will refer to this area as *skills* or "S." For skill training, the technologies located in the center of the continuum are most appropriate, and the facilitator must not only have an understanding of the skill itself but must also know how to use these technologies.

Finally, affective learning includes the development of awareness, the discovery of preferences, and the exploration (and possible change) of attitudes. This type of learning is best initiated by highly participative activities in which the content of the session is drawn from the participants. To best remind us of what this type of learning is about, we will refer to it as *awareness/attitudes* or "A."

These different training objectives can be illustrated as shown in the figure on the following page.[2] This leads us into the second mistake most often made in designing training modules.

Relating Activities to Goals/Objectives

It is imperative that facilitators be clear about how much of the content of a training module is to come from outside the participants (to be imparted *to* them) and how much is to consist of drawing content *from* the participants and using it, exploring it, and processing it to promote increased understanding and new learning. The following check list can help in selecting design components that are appropriate.

K	S	A
Knowledge, Concepts, Cognitive Input and Memorization	**Physical and Behavioral Skills**	**Awareness, Discovery of Preferences, Exploration of Attitudes**
New ideas Procedures Points of view Models (teaching about the model)	Practice Application of ideas Models (procedural, applying the process) Procedures	Personal biases Preferences Unique interpretations Applications of ideas Models (used to clarify personal applications) Processes

1. How much *involvement* do you want from the participants? How much do you need to accomplish the training objectives? (If none, maybe all you need are good readings, lectures, platform skills, audiovisuals).
2. How important is disclosure? discovery? self-understanding? feedback? (For example, these would be critical if you were preparing the participants to be managers.)
3. How much of the participants' *content* do you need to achieve the training objective?

The primary thing to remember in applying all this is to be honest about what you are trying to do. The mistake that facilitators most often make is using activities such as questioning, role plays, instruments, and structured experiences—which open up the participants—and then *not using* what is generated: the participants' observations, feelings, and insights. If you want to teach the participants a particular content, it is not a good idea to initiate a structured experience, generate their feelings and ideas, and then ignore these and lecture. It is not a good idea to solicit their opinions and then edit them so that they only reflect what you had in mind. When you open up or stir up the participants, generating their ideas and feelings, they expect you to work with them. We also have seen trainers ask questions of the participants and then ignore the participants' responses or, perhaps worse, edit or rephrase them so that the trainers can create a list that says what they want it to say. The rule that is being violated here can be phrased in several ways: "Do not ask the question if you do not want to deal with the answer" or "Do not start what you are not prepared to finish." The following illustration[3] may help to reinforce this concept.

Presenting Skills . . . . Facilitating Skills

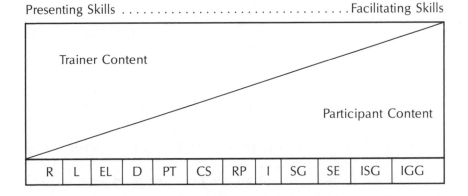

This does not mean that that a training program cannot include cognitive components as well as highly participative ones. Any or all of the training technologies may be appropriate in some part of the training design; the key is to structure each *module* to achieve what you want to achieve *at that time and in that sequence.* In an overall training design, there might well be some combination of modules that focus on cognitive input (knowledge/concepts), skills practice (skills), and high participant participation

---

[2,3]These versions of the involvement continuum were developed by Phyliss Cooke, Ph.D., for University Associates.

(awareness/attitudes). If one is clear about the overall training objectives for the program, one then can determine the objective for each *session,* and then the objective for each separate *module.* Again, the key is to be clear about what the goal of *each module* or each segment of the training design is. One module may be designed to impart basic concepts, the next one may be designed to draw out the participants' reactions to and experiences with these concepts, and the next may be to have the participants create a pictorial model of a process related to the concepts. If each module is congruent (i.e., the training technology or design component is congruent with the training objective), the modules can be sequenced in an order that makes sense.

The second key is to sequence the modules so that the participants are not confused or frustrated by the apparent discrepancy between the stated goals and what is actually being done. Such dissonance can impede or block learning. The training design is simply a blueprint for how *time* is to be used to accomplish the training objective. Knowing clearly what you are trying to do, doing it simply and in the most appropriate manner (selecting the right vehicle), and sequencing modules to build from one type of learning toward another is what good design is all about.

Identifying Participant Goals

A closely related set of skills involves helping the participants to identify and clarify their own goals as they relate to the stated goals of the event. It is important that training activities be carried out in reference to highly specific goals that are related to the behavior of the participants. Each participant should have something to work for during the training experience. The expectation check at the beginning of the training program can help to serve this purpose.

Being Sensitive to Participant Response

A fourth set of skills in designing experiential educational events relates to sensitivity to participant response. The facilitator learns to anticipate how participants are likely to react to particular components of the design and becomes adept at anticipating the cumulative effects of the design. The facilitator should be able to make some probability statements about the receptivity of participants to particular learning experiences at a particular point in the event. Part of this sensitivity involves acquaintanceship with the client system. It is important that the facilitator be able to know how participants are likely to react to particular structured experiences and to particular foci within the overall experience. For example, if the training event is to begin with a nonverbal activity, how much tension is this likely to create in this particular set of participants at this particular point in its development? How are the same participants likely to react to a similar activity after they have been together in a retreat setting for two days? Sensitivity to the probable participant response is developed from experience with a variety of learning activities, with a variety of clients, and with a great deal of staff discussion of experiences in similar learning situations.

Timing

Sequencing and the planning of time are critical elements in training design. A training design is actually a blueprint of how the available time will be used. In designing each training module, it is crucial to take into consideration the time that will be needed for orientation, maintenance, instructions, distribution of materials, questions and answers, processing, etc., and to *subtract that from the total time available* when planning time for structured interventions such as lecturettes, discussions, case studies, instruments, structured experiences, and so on. A good way to think about this is in terms of what Phyliss Cooke calls "the dance," a series of four steps that take place in each training session, no matter how long the total event is.

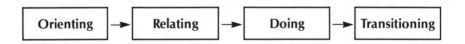

I. *Orienting.* When participants enter the training room, the first task is to help them to "get their heads into (or back into) the room." At the beginning of a training event, this requires a good deal of effort. At the beginning of subsequent days or after breaks, participants may need to be helped to clear away their outside realities before they can focus on the training. It may be wise, for example, to ask if anyone had trouble in traffic that morning or if anything important or exciting happened during the lunch break. Remember, you cannot run a race until the horses are at the gate.

The amount of time required for this step will depend on the location of the module in the overall design. It no doubt will take longer for the participants to align themselves at the beginning of the first day than it will at the beginning of the second day. Similarly, the beginning of a day and the beginning of a module after a meal break probably will require more time than the beginning of a module after a short break. If things are running smoothly, the latter may require only a minute or two, whereas the task of opening the initial session may take from several minutes to an hour or more.

II. *Relating.* The next step is to establish task and relationship orientations, to deal with the participants' "what" and "who" questions (generally not verbalized), to help them to buy in psychologically. The "what" includes an overview of the event and a clarification of the training objectives or goals and the roles of the facilitator and the participants. The "who" means who they are and the establishment of norms for working together. The features, advantages, and benefits of the session can be described briefly. If there is resistance, it needs to be explored. A getting-acquainted, ice-breaker, or warm-up activity in this step can provide data about whether the participants are ready to proceed. (This is discussed in more detail in the next chapter, in the section on getting-acquainted activities.) During this step, the facilitator needs to convince the participants that something important is going to happen before they take their next significant break.

What actually happens during steps I and II is described in more detail in the section entitled "Opening the Session" in the next chapter of this book.

III. *Doing.* The next task is to work on achieving the training objective—the knowledge, skills, or awareness component and the core content. This may include a lecture, a discussion, a list-building process, a structured experience, or any of the other design components, as appropriate. As we stated previously, the time allotted for this step should allow for questions and answers, rearrangement of seating, processing discussions, and whatever else might occur that is related to the task objective. Participants should understand their task objectives during this phase so that they know what they are working toward.

IV. *Transitioning.* The final step in each training module is to actually work toward transition, the transfer of learning from the training setting to the real world. One cannot expect the participants to complete a training module and automatically know how or be willing to "do" something. The facilitator needs to build toward transition in the design. The sequence should be smooth and logical, and new content should *not* be added toward the end. The focus here is on integration and application; typical structures are subgrouping and practice teams. In the beginning and middle of the training event, the transition will be directed toward the next module, toward preparing to accomplish the next learning objectives.

Transition also is the final objective of the overall training event, so adequate time should be planned at the end of the event to focus on the issue of transition of the overall learnings to the participants' real-life situations.

One aspect of transition that often is neglected is the need for reinforcement and support in applying new learnings and new skills and in practicing new behaviors. If participants will not be receiving support in their work or home environments, they can make contracts with one another (usually in pairs or trios) to telephone or write to report successes, ask for advice, and provide reinforcement for one another. The facilitator also may be available after the training has ended to counsel and provide "strokes."

What training designers must remember is that the clock does not drive the design; the designer *uses* time. The task of designing is to decide how the time will be divided into chunks (modules) within each session and each day. Each module consists of a different dance—the four steps of orienting, relating, doing, and transitioning—built around a specific training objective. Step three may consist of more than one design component, but all parts of the module should have the same content focus or learning objective. The figure that follows may help to illustrate this concept.

	Day 1	Day 2	Day 3	Day 4
Morning	I II III	I II III	I II III	III IV
Afternoon	I II III IV	I II III IV	III	IV

The question for the designer is how to allocate the time within each module and within each day so that they lead to the final transition. It is important not to run out of time and shortchange or skip step IV at the end of each day. It is critical that step IV not be shortchanged or skipped in the final day or final session. If you miss the transfer, the training program may well have been a wasted effort.

The following is an example of how to begin looking at the time available for a day of training.

1 day = 7½ hours = 450 minutes

Minus: 4 breaks at 10 minutes each
(2 in a.m., 2 in p.m.):   40 minutes
Lunch: 75 minutes
Slippage: 30 minutes
_____
145 minutes

450 minutes - 145 minutes = 305 minutes

It is always necessary to plan in time for slippage, which can be anything from people coming in late and needing to be "caught up" to the inevitable "side trips" resulting from questions and comments during discussions and activities.

This leaves not 450 minutes in which to achieve steps I through IV, but 305 minutes. Depending on what day of training this is and, therefore, how much time steps I, II, and IV are likely to require, the designer can determine how much time is available for step III, the knowledge, skills, or awareness components—which generally are thought of as the learning part of the training. In fact, if one is designing for the final day, the time allocated for the transition phase may be equal to or greater than the time allocated for the knowledge, skills, or awareness phase. Any of the design components may be selected to effect the transition as long as they end with questions such as "So what?" or "Now what?" or "How will you *use* this in . . . ?"

In planning both time and sequence, it is helpful to block out the days and modules visually (as we have done previously in this section), to enter the steps required in each module, and to compute how much time will be available for each before selecting the design components to be used in each step and each module. In this way, one is less likely to plan an activity that one simply does not have the time to execute properly.

Sequencing

The task of sequencing is one of the most important sets of skills in training design. Learning events are not put together in a random way; it is important that the facilitator be able to see the impact of one particular training component on the one that immediately follows it. Sometimes the objective is to close things down; at other times the objective may be to open things up in order for the next training module to be more effective. One of the major purposes of this book is to expand the group facilitator's awareness of sequencing considerations in training designs.

Every component of the design should fit into an ordered scheme that begins with the learning objectives and results in the attainment of the goals of the event. This means that *each activity* within the training experience *should build from the previous sequence of activities and toward the next one.*

Balance also should be considered in the sequencing so that the participants are not overloaded with either cognitive or experiential components. Activities should be varied in terms of type, length, and intensity. Within content blocks, activities should progress from less difficult to more difficult, from less risky to more risky, from easy concepts to more complex ones.

There also should be a balance between tense moments and relaxed ones. Although some tension or discomfort may be required for change to take place, there must be some comfort so that people can integrate their learnings and share their insights. Because of this, skills should be demonstrated by the facilitators or selected participants before they are practiced and practiced before they are actually used.

Sometimes it is important in the sequence to have thematic material that runs throughout all the components of the training design, thus allowing for the processing of a variety of events and experiences against the same theoretical model.

Even the breaks and the meals should be planned strategically, and the effect of the interactions within breaks and meals needs to be anticipated as one plans for the events that follow. It is ideal if participants can digest their learnings and practice their new skills between sessions (during breaks). Toward this end, they should be encouraged to go to lunch and dinner with other participants in the training event. Many participants may be sluggish after meals, so it is a good idea to plan an energizing activity when regrouping to get them back into the training mood.

Balance and pacing also should be considered in planning the activities of the staff members so they that do not become fatigued or burn out.

Collaborating with Other Facilitators

If two or more people will be co-facilitating an event, it is best if they co-design it. If this is not practical or possible for some reason, they at least must discuss the overall purpose of the design and the methods that will be employed. How will facilitation be shared?

Will there be a leader or will the task of facilitation be shared equally? How much freedom does each trainer have to make changes in the design, the timing, etc.?

In our experience, it usually is more effective and efficient for one facilitator to accept responsibility for the initial design of the training event and to work with other facilitators to edit the design to make it more relevant to the learning needs of the participants in light of the goals of the event. It is expensive to bring together a group of facilitators to build a design from the ground up. It is true that when staff members create a design themselves, they are more likely to have a sense of investment, involvement, and psychological ownership in what is planned. They are likely to approach the implementation of the design with more vigor. It is also true, however, that training staffs ordinarily do not have a great deal of time to prepare for a particular event. We find it useful to have an initial, tentative design that the staff will edit rather than to build one from the beginning.

One of the major problems in design has centered around collaboration skills. Many group facilitators have their own favorite ways of doing things and sometimes are reluctant to collaborate in experimenting with other teaching procedures. It is sadly ironic that trainers often become locked into particular ways of working and violate their own norms of experimentation and innovation. For this and other reasons, co-designers need to process the process. It is to be expected that different people may have different orientations and different levels of energy. Discussing the process and sharing points of view can be a highly beneficial and educational experience for any trainer.

Modifying Designs

Another important set of skills involves modifying designs while the training event is in progress. While producing a plan of activities for fostering learning, there is no way that the trainers can anticipate all the responses of the participants and all the real-time concerns that become relevant. Trainers need to develop the ability to change the learning design while it is running. This involves taking data from the participants about their own needs at a particular stage of the event's development and finding appropriate alternatives to what was planned. When the trainers discover that what was planned back in the staff meeting no longer makes sense in terms of what is happening now, they need to be able to redirect the learning experience without becoming threatened by their lack of anticipation of participant response.

Skill in designing training events involves learning how to make one's goals highly explicit and specific, learning to anticipate how particular participants are likely to respond to various learning activities, learning to put training design components together in meaningful ways, developing the ability to collaborate noncompetitively with other facilitators in producing designs, and developing the ability to redirect the learning experience while it is in progress.

5

Major Dimensions of Design

Several major dimensions will be discussed in this chapter to guide the facilitator in the process of designing a training event.

Goals

As has been indicated previously, it is critical for the facilitator to know the priorities and learning goals of a particular training event, in order to be able to specify them clearly and to be able to keep the learning event goal directed at all times. All proposed activities should be related to the goals of the training and should enhance attainment of the learning objectives. It also is important that the facilitator be able to help participants to clarify their own goals if they are unclear. Every person in the workshop should have some understanding of why he or she is there.

Opening the Session

Sufficient time must be allotted at the beginning of the training event for the facilitator to perform the following opening tasks:

- Allow the participants time to become settled in the room. Then welcome the participants.
- Introduce the event, stating its objectives or goals and what the participants might gain from it. The common purpose in a training event is the training objective.
- Introduce the training staff and explain their qualifications and roles (perhaps their orientations).

- Provide a brief overview of the event, session by session or day by day—what the group will accomplish in the time available. It is important that the participants understand what they are going to do and why they are going to do it.
- Delineate rules and discuss expected norms (the concepts of trust, experimentation, risk taking, voluntariness, etc.). Clarify operating procedures and explain staff expectations.
- Attend to "housekeeping": Announce the schedule (starting and ending times, lunch times, and breaks) and check to see that all participants can adhere to it. Announce whether drinks and refreshments will be available and whether participants can leave their seats to get them at any time during the sessions. Discuss the tone of the session (formal or informal) and the expected style of dress. Announce whether smoking is permitted in the training room and, if not, where people may go to smoke. Request that participants clean up after themselves, and so on.
- Conduct a getting-acquainted activity or, at least, have each participant announce his or her name and any other information that would be *helpful or useful* in this initial phase.
- Check expectations: The period of getting acquainted with the staff and an invitation to open up should be followed by the establishment of some expectations for the training event. Participants can be asked "What do you expect to get out of this training event?" The more clear and specific the responses are, the better. People typically ask questions such as "Are we going to deal with (some subject)?" The participants' expectations and desires then can be checked against those of the staff. Any inconsistencies or blocks can be discussed. In some cases, it may be possible to modify the design to include material that is important to the participants or that will help to achieve their goals.

All these introductory functions should be clarified and completed before any content is introduced into the training event. Many of these functions will need to be performed *at the beginning of each day,* and several of them may need to be done *at the beginning of each session* (after breaks, meals, etc.).

Getting Acquainted and Other Orienting Activities

It is necessary to do something to help people to become oriented to the other group members and to the training. Most adults orient in terms of *what*—"What are we here for?, What is the task?" A few are *who* oriented—"Who are these people and what are they about?" Facilitators who orient in terms of the "what" tend not to plan well for those who orient in terms of the "who," and vice versa, but both need to be covered. In skills and awareness training, the participants need more "who." "What" may be sufficient for pure content training. The training designers should know enough about the participant group to plan for them.

A primary thing to consider in designing a getting-acquainted activity is what its purpose is. Trainers frequently confuse getting-acquainted activities with ice breakers, energizers, and activities designed to introduce conceptual material. The following listing may help to clear up this confusion.

- *Getting acquainted.* These activities help the group members to get to know one another and to "warm up" for the events that are to follow.
- *Ice breakers.* These activities help the group members to break through existing, self-imposed barriers or boundaries. They force or encourage participants to *do* things in different ways. The intended result is to loosen up both behaviors and attitudes.
- *Forming subgroups.* These simple activities provide a variety of ways to divide the learning group into smaller subgroups.
- *Expectations of learners.* Some activities are designed to elicit the expectations, goals, or hopes of the participants in regard to the training event so that these can be compared with those of the facilitator.
- *Building trust/building norms of openness.* Some activities are designed to create trust and a climate of openness and learning within the group. They typically involve sharing and a moderate level of risk taking; they may include the giving and receiving of feedback.

- *Energizers.* These "recharge" the group members when energy is low.
- *Dealing with blocks to learning.* There are activities that are designed to deal with situations in which learning is blocked through the interference of other dynamics, conscious or unconscious, in the group.
- *Evaluating learning/group Process.* These help individuals to evaluate what is taking place within a learning group.

The purpose of a getting-acquainted activity is to generate enough information of a high enough quality to establish the desired climate, to enable people to feel safe, to start the process, to get people on board with one another and with the task and ready to do the task. The sequence, then, is familiarity, risk, and transition to task.

In designing or selecting a getting-acquainted activity, it is a good idea to keep people's needs in mind. If the participants are meeting and sharing with one another for the first time, they will be experiencing some anxiety. It is difficult for people in these circumstances to effectively participate in a *sequential* activity. Before their turn, they may not hear or remember what others said because they are thinking about what they will say. After their turn, they may be able to listen to others or they may be worrying about how they did and how they were perceived. Having participants take turns in random sequence can help here. Another way to ease the stress is to avoid having participants stand up to talk while others are seated. Activities that call for the participants to share information and prepare in dyads, triads, or quartets and then report out or introduce one another can be highly effective. Designs that call for the participants to mingle also are useful.

If there is some acquaintanceship and some trust and support established in the group, a sequential activity may be easier to manage. In general, getting acquainted is a stressful activity. If it is "heavy" for the group members, it should be followed by reacting (processing) time or by something equally heavy to support the participants' moods.

It would be premature to conduct an activity designed to build trust and openness before the group members have had a chance to become at least minimally acquainted with one another. Similarly, an "energizer" is not needed if things are moving along and people are involved. Even worse would be to introduce an activity as a "getting-acquainted" or "icebreaker" intervention when its real purpose is to interject some content into the participants' consciousness. One should never begin a high-risk activity at the beginning of an event, when the participants have not yet become acquainted and established some trust and norms of risk taking. This is another reason why it is important to be clear about what one is doing and not to confuse getting-acquainted activities with awareness or skills activities. This type of manipulation is almost always perceived and resented by the participants. Remembering two things can help to prevent this from happening: (a) know specifically what your objective is and be honest about what you are trying to achieve; and (b) attend to steps I and II of "the dance" (to whatever degree is needed) before you attempt to execute step III.

Facilitator Participation

A question that often is asked is "Should the facilitator(s) be included in the getting-acquainted activity?" The answer may be yes or no. Including the facilitator affects role clarity (including the facilitator's subsequent ability to make unilateral decisions). It is difficult to say "I am one of the group members" and then follow it with "O.K., you guys, listen up!" Also, if dyads or subgroups are working on a preliminary task for a getting-acquainted activity, the facilitator may want to take that time to prepare flip charts or other materials. The decision to participate or not must be based on the needs of the participants (do they really need to hear you?), the training objectives, and the facilitator's planned role in the training process (e.g., lecturer or director versus fellow participant in experiential/ exploratory learning).

Time for Ongoing Maintenance

As the event proceeds, time should be allotted to processing what is happening, with the expectation that participants will have questions or comments. What one does *not* want to do is plan the schedule so tightly that participants feel rushed or pushed. It is important to allow time for participants to explore what is happening to them. Facilitators often discover that the group is going in a direction that is not planned, although it is productive. In such a situation, the facilitators need the flexibility to modify the design to accommodate the learning needs of the group.

Time also should be allowed for periodic feedback from the participants to check on how the design is working. There must be adequate time at the end of structured experiences, instruments, and other activities to make sense of and reinforce the learnings. Finally, time must be scheduled at the end of each day and at the end of the workshop for summary and evaluation.

Norms

The most meaningful expectations for the facilitator to establish and maintain are those of strategic openness, experimentation, participation, responsibility, and sensitivity to self and others. Strategic openness means avoiding the extremes of being dysfunctionally open or of colluding with other people not to talk about taboo topics. Experimentation means trying new behaviors within the workshop. Participation involves helping to make it happen for oneself and for others. Responsibility means taking responsibility for one's own learning, not expecting to be spoon-fed by the facilitator. (This might be translated as: "It is the facilitator's job to teach, but it is my job to learn.") Sensitivity to self and others means that participants should be aware of the feelings that they are experiencing and that they should also attempt to be aware of the readiness of other people to get involved with them in open interchange of here-and-now data.

Voluntariness

A major goal of experiential education is to increase freedom rather than to coerce people into activities in which they otherwise might not participate voluntarily. This is true especially if persons attend the training event involuntarily. Some people react with a great deal of tension to activities involving physical touch, and they should not be required or unduly pressured to participate in such activities. The silent member of the intensive small group may be tyrannized by other group members into saying things that the person does not want to reveal, and the principle of voluntariness may be violated. Thus, in designing the experience, one must be sensitive to the needs of some participants not to involve themselves in every single activity. The best design allows the participants to make conscious choices about their levels of involvement by ensuring that activities provide a variety of meaningful roles.

Investment and Involvement

In designing an interactive training event, it is important to plan not to have passive audiences at any time; every participant needs to have something to do all the time during the formal sessions. If there is going to be a lecture, the facilitator may stress active listening. If a structured experience is to be used, roles should be assigned so that every person has something to do that contributes to his or her learning within the context of the experience. (Some participants can be designated as observers, provided with observation guides, and requested to provide feedback at the conclusion of the activity.) During a group activity, all participants should have the task of noticing and analyzing process dynamics. The important thing is that, from the beginning, each participant is led to accept responsibility for learning within the training context and that ample opportunity is provided to act out this responsibility through participation.

Pacing

It is important for the training staff to keep things moving and to avoid passivity and boredom, but facilitators also must be sensitive to the effects of fatigue on the participants. One can design a training event that has such a breakneck pace that participants come out of the event having been overloaded with stimuli. Some time is needed for people to think things out, and free time should be built into the design simply to give people an escape from the heavy work demands of the event.

As a general rule, when things begin to drag, it probably is time to make a change. Sometimes the most effective change simply is to point out the process that is emerging and to help participants to understand its nature. In a group meeting, for example, if there is a long silence, it may be important for the group to deal with the responsibility of the individual participants to avoid dysfunctional silence. If the pace is characterized by frequent interventions on the part of the facilitator, it may lead to dependency on the part of the participants and they may come to expect the facilitator to make things happen. The pace of the events within a laboratory, then, should be dictated by the probable fatigue effect, the necessity to provide plenty of time for adequate processing of data, and the need not to reinforce dependency on the facilitators.

Data

Data in the form of thoughts, feelings, and behavior are always present in the training milieu. Sometimes during an event, participants may comment that nothing appears to be happening, but often this simply is evidence that they are not monitoring the complexity of the emerging process. It is important to recognize and talk about whatever is actually happening and to try to relate dynamics to the focus of the training. The data-generating techniques that have been discussed previously can be highly effective in focusing particular here-and-now phenomena toward the learning goals of the event.

Flexibility

The designer of the training experience must plan to use maximum data from the event itself to modify the design so that it meets the learning needs of the participants. This means being open to (in fact, planning) to change the design during the event. We find it useful to overdesign workshops in the sense that, at any given point, several options are being considered. Based on the information available about the participant group, certain possible design modifications can be planned ahead of time, and the facilitators need to have the skills to consider others on site as the need arises. This implies a lot of coordination (i.e., staffing time), especially if staff members are new to one another. In effect, this consideration of several options at any point becomes a kind of on-the-job training for designing learning events.

Flexibility also means avoiding "packaged" designs that are preplanned and that do not account adequately for the responsiveness of particular participants or that do not lend themselves to being customized appropriately.

Structure

There are two aspects to the structure of a training design. The first is the visible part: what people can see that tells them what is going to happen. This includes posted agendas, seating arrangements, pens, notebooks, flip charts, etc. There should be a balance of visible structure at the beginning of a training event. Too little may cause concern; the participants need to see that something is going to happen. Too much could stifle individual contributions. People want to have input into their own learning; they want to affect the amount and type of structure. In general, it is desirable to have some visible structure at the beginning of an event. This should be geared to the participants and must be congruent with the system in which the training is taking place and with the training objective.

The second aspect of structure is the amount. High structure in design may not require high visibility. There can be a great deal of structure in the design, with preplanned activities, materials, etc., without it being highly visible. Participants generally want and need less structure as they begin to take responsibility for their own learning. For this reason, there is more visible structure in knowledge/ concepts training and less in working with the content of the participants generated by experiential learning.

The following illustration shows the relationships between visibility and amount of structure in training design.

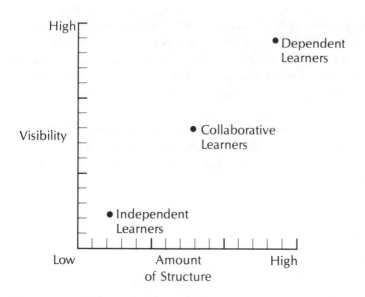

Content, Experiential and Conceptual Input

The facilitator must always plan to check the content of the training against the needs of the participants. For example, if the group is experiencing conflict, a relaxation activity at the beginning of a session may make it difficult for the members to get back into dealing with the negative issues. The facilitator needs to be aware of inclusion issues in the group, developing norms, levels of participation, task and maintenance roles of members, dominance, patterns of influence, types of influence or sources of power, verbal and nonverbal behaviors, uses of humor, treatment of silent members, decision-making processes, commitment to group process, atmosphere, and so on.

Another consideration in initiating content is the trainer's group-facilitation skills. In short, do not start things you cannot finish. Do not attempt to run activities that you have not experienced, tried out, or observed.

A third consideration is to be aware of your own preferences and prejudices and to consider whether they fit with the needs of the participants. It is important that the data and the techniques used in the training be relevant to the participants' training needs and interests. It is highly desirable that the content be related to the participants' occupations or primary concerns and that it be locally relevant whenever possible. This is particularly true in skills training and in leadership- and management-development workshops, in which the content of the activities needs to parallel closely the kinds of concerns and problems that participants ordinarily face in their work. A number of data-generating techniques can be employed within the training sessions to ensure that the content of the learning design is relevant to the participants as they are experiencing it. The following are several useful strategies.

- Participants can be asked to make notes to themselves about particular feelings they are experiencing, thoughts they are thinking, persons to whom they are reacting, and so on. One useful technique is the "think-feel" card, on which participants are instructed to record their reactions at any particular point. On one side they are to write a sentence beginning with "I think," and on the other side they are to write a sentence beginning with "I feel." This process very often heightens the participants' willingness to share these reactions with others.

- A useful intervention is to form dyads and to ask the members of each pair to interview each other with regard to their reactions to a particular issue, event, or piece of behavioral datum at a given time. Often we ask people to use this as an exercise in active listening. Ordinarily, the interviewers should not make notes but should frequently paraphrase what they hear, to make certain that they are not translating in terms of their own reality rather than being sensitive to the phenomenological systems of the persons being interviewed.

- A list of concerns can be generated rapidly on a flip chart or chalkboard. Such a list might include issues or problems facing the group at any given moment, controversial topics or persons, etc. Participants can be asked to rank-order the list according to some criterion such as urgency or influence. Often it is useful to ask participants first to perform a ranking independently to establish their own points of view and then to divide them into small groups, each to develop a consensus ranking of the material.

- Questionnaires can be developed that include multiple-choice items, rating scales, open-ended questions, and so on. These can be used prior to or within the training event to generate data for participant learning. It is important that participants take the responsibility to process the data, and it may be desirable to post the statistical results so that the group can analyze itself.
- It sometimes is helpful for a group to look back on its own history to analyze how it has used its time. A list of topics that have constituted the group's agenda in past meetings can be generated, and the amount of energy that has been expended on any given item can be discussed. Sometimes a group discovers that an inordinate amount of energy has been expended on particular concerns and that it may be able to use its time more efficiently.
- Videotaping is an excellent technique. It is extremely difficult to recapture much of the data generated in a learning event by depending on memory alone, and the advantages of videotape—with instant and repeated playback—are obvious. Nonverbal data can be highly focused by the use of this medium, and it often is very useful in teaching process awareness.
- A group can look at its own development at any given moment through a problem-solving method called force-field analysis. A lecturette in the 1973 *Annual,* "Kurt Lewin's 'Force Field Analysis'" (Spier, 1973), describes this process.
- Occasionally, teaching the distinction between content and process is made easier by using activities whose content is obviously a simulation of "real-world" concerns. In an experiential training event, the task sometimes becomes so seductive that the group fails to look effectively at its own internal functioning. Such a process orientation can be generated rapidly through the use of an activity that focuses on interpersonal dynamics.

Participants frequently enter a training event unaware of their own incompetence in certain areas, but also unaware of their competence. One of the trainer's primary tasks is to help the participants to become conscious of the areas in which they can benefit from growth and change and also to help them to become conscious of the areas in which they have strengths and skills in order to capitalize on them and expand or refine them.

The Experiential Learning Cycle

In our opinion, the basis of adult training is experiential learning. It is true that this type of learning takes more time than purely didactic methods, but with experiential learning things come to life. The learning cannot translate directly from the facilitator's head to the participant's head; it needs to be translated into the participant's frame of reference. In experiential learning a person engages in some activity, looks back at the activity critically, abstracts some useful insight from the analysis, and puts the result to work through a change in behavior. The key here is change. Awareness and understanding are fine, but they may not result in behavioral change; *learning* occurs when individuals adjust or modify their behavior. Thus, awareness and understanding are only part of learning. The facilitator's job is to guide the learning process and to provide a sound theoretical base from which the participants can obtain insights and models that they can use in guiding their behavior.

There are several models that describe how learning occurs (see Palmer, 1981); all state that learners move through a series of steps involving discovery, formulating and producing new behavior, and generalizing to the real world with the help of a trainer/facilitator. Our preferred description of how this process occurs (or should occur) was first published in the 1975 *Annual* and was expanded in the 1980 *Annual* (Pfeiffer & Jones, 1980). The model is presented in detail in Chapter 1 of *Using Structured Experiences in Human Resource Development,* the first book in this Training Technologies series. The summary below will serve as a reminder of the five stages of the model as a critical element in training design.

The Experiential Learning Cycle

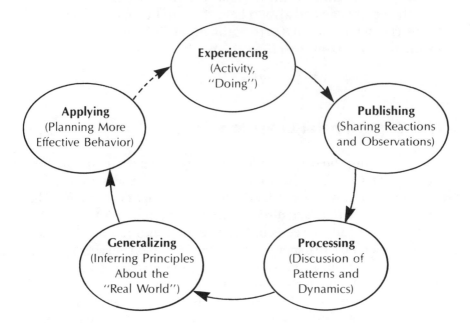

Experiencing

The process starts with experiencing. The participant becomes in-volved in an activity; he or she acts or behaves in some way or does, performs, observes, sees, or says something. This initial experience is the basis for the entire process.

Techniques that facilitate the experiencing phase are as follows:

- making products
- creating art
- writing skits
- role playing
- transactions
- problem solving

- feedback
- self-disclosure
- guided imagery
- choosing
- nonverbal communication

- analysis
- bargaining
- planning
- competing
- collaborating
- confronting

Useful structures include individuals, small groups, subgroups, total groups, dyads, triads, and intergroups.

Publishing

Following the experience itself, it becomes important for the participants to share or "publish" their reactions and observations with others who have either experienced or observed the same activity.

Techniques that aid publishing include:

- recording data
- free discussion
- subgroup sharing
- posting, round-robin listing
- averaging
- go around
- whip

Processing

Sharing one's reactions is only the first step. An essential—and often neglected—part of the cycle is the necessary integration of this sharing. The dynamics that emerged in the activity are compared, explored, discussed, and evaluated (processed) with other participants. This is a crucial step in the learning cycle.

Helpful processing techniques are:

- observers
- rating scales
- themes
- completing sentences
- questionnaires
- adjectives
- discussing questions (what/how)
- interveners
- key terms
- nominations

Generalizing

Flowing logically from the processing step is the need to develop principles or extract generalizations from the experience. Stating learnings in this way can help participants to further define, clarify, and elaborate them.

Generalizing techniques include:

- writing statements
- key words
- completing sentences
- individual analysis

Applying

The final step in the cycle is to plan applications of the principles derived from the experience. The experiential process is not complete until a new learning or discovery is used and tested behaviorally. This is the "experimental" part of the model. Applying, of course, becomes an experience in itself, and with new experience, the cycle begins again.

Techniques that aid in facilitating the applying phase are as follows:

- goal setting
- contracting
- interviewing
- subgrouping
- practice sessions

Processing of Data

Perhaps our most firm commitment in a training design is to make absolutely certain that there is adequate time for processing the data that are generated by particular design components. It is in the processing activity itself, which immediately follows every learning experience, that the participants' learnings and insights are tied together, the question of "so what?" is answered, and the transfer of learning is bolstered. If human resource development is, in fact, training for everyday work, it is important that we heighten the probability that such transfer will take place. Processing involves the talking through of behavioral and feeling data that emerge in a particular activity and then discussing the learning and action implications. A cardinal rule here, then, is: Do not generate more data during the activities and input stages than can be talked through during the processing stages. We are convinced that it is both dangerous and unethical to leave large portions of data hanging that might be integrated in dysfunctional ways within the consciousness of a given individual. The importance of providing sufficient air time within the training design to sort out and share reactions to particular events cannot be overemphasized.

A number of structures have been developed to help participants to process data. The following is a partial listing of these designs.

- Participants and trainers can be used as *observers* in some structured experiences. It sometimes is useful to provide process-observation recording forms on which the observer may make notes during the event. Sometimes we will interrupt an event to hear reports from the process observers. Occasionally we have several process observers who form a discussion panel after the event to pool their observations. We often incorporate into the design the option for any number of participants to take turns functioning as external process observers. Occasionally we set up a particular structured experience so that the participants will stop at a predetermined point to process their reactions up to that point.

- A facilitator can be used as a *consultant* to a particular group that is accomplishing a task or working on a particular problem within the workshop. This may be done on a continual basis—that is, a consultant may be requested at any time while a group is working—or the timing of the interventions of the process consultant can be preplanned. Participants also can be trained to perform this function.

- After an activity on listening and process observation, *participants can be encouraged to use one another as consultants* in dyadic relationships that emerge during the training event. If two participants are having difficulty communicating with each other, they might seek out a third party to help them to listen more effectively. This can be very useful training that can be transferred to the back-home situation. It is important for a participant to develop the ability to play the role of process consultant rather than to be a person who mediates conflict or takes sides on the content of a particular issue.

- *The group-on-group, or fishbowl, design* is one of the most powerful processing techniques. In this design, one group sits in the center of the room while the members of the other group(s) sit around it, outside its boundaries, and observe what the first group is doing (discussing, processing, etc.).

What lends it potency is that the group operating within the fishbowl is under considerable pressure to work hard at focusing on process. In addition, the group in the center can use other participants as consultants for its own internal functioning.

- To increase the air time for individual participants, it may be useful to *divide a large group into a number of small groups* (three to six members each) for rapid processing of data. This can be structured so that there are reporters who will give brief synopses to the total group at a predetermined time of the major themes that emerged in the subgroups. Subgrouping gives many people a chance to be heard and understood in less time, and it can heighten the getting-acquainted process.

- A *circle of chairs* can be placed in the center of the room with the ground rule that an individual who wishes to speak about what is occurring must occupy one of the chairs in the center. Each speaker leaves the center and returns to the audience once he or she has finished speaking. This has the effect of including any number of participants in open interchange. It is particularly useful when working with very large groups of people. A drawback of this technique, of course, is that people who are more reticent or who are not risk takers may be unwilling to participate.

- Many people find that the transfer of learning is easier if they receive support in making action plans and commitments and in practicing new behaviors. In looking back at the process of learning in the experiential-training experience, participants sometimes can focus on particular things that they have been doing by *developing contracts,* or promises, with one another that they attempt to fulfill within a specified time. The members of the contracting pairs or groups agree to telephone one another or write in order to receive assistance and reinforcement and to report progress. This process of contracting can lead to highly useful applications in the back-home setting. We sometimes incorporate within the helping-pair design the writing of contracts for back-home application of specific learnings, with planned follow-through built into the contract. Participants also can be encouraged to make contracts with others in their work settings to practice and receive feedback on specific behaviors when they go back to the job. The nature of the learning will dictate whether or not this might be helpful.

The bridging and application processes work best after people have thought about their old patterns and behaviors and developed new frames of reference; thus, it is important to allow time for the processing of relevant segments of the training as it progresses. This also allows the participants to put it all together before the final application step.

A final part of the facilitator's task in helping participants to plan how to apply their learnings from the training is to help them to prepare what they will do if their new behaviors meet resistance in their back-home settings.

The next chapter contains some sample sequences and explanations of the rationale behind them.

Sample Design Sequences

There is, we believe, an organic sequence of activities that is useful to consider in designing human-interaction training events. This section will delineate this sequence in terms of the design components discussed previously. Although the emphasis often is different, the flow of activities within different kinds of learning programs overlaps somewhat. To serve as examples, we primarily will consider the design of two kinds of training events that often are developed by group facilitators: personal growth and executive-development workshops.

Personal Growth Designs

In a personal growth setting, although there are definite learning goals that involve the use of skills in their accomplishment, there is less emphasis on skill building than there is in many other types of workshops. The three key goals in personal growth are developing awareness of self and others, learning how to give and receive feedback constructively, and increasing skills in interpersonal relationships. Toward these ends, skills in listening, expressing, and responding are needed, and their development must be integrated into the design of the experience. These three skills will be discussed more thoroughly in the next section. This is one of the areas in which these two basic concepts overlap.

The flow of learning that is implied in the tabulation that follows suggests a sequence of events leading to the optimum use of time in personal growth. These things need to be done in a logical flow, from getting acquainted to going home. A variety of structures can be utilized to effect this sequence, which is relevant both to retreats and to spaced meetings. The sequence is not the design of an ideal training event so much as it is an outline of the learning needs of participants in a personal growth context.

Executive-Development Designs

Another genre of training is called "management development," "leadership development," "executive development," or even "communication skills." The events generally are described as conferences, workshops, or seminars, and although there may be some distinctions in content among them, they all focus on skill building and conceptual development through experiential methods. They differ from personal growth laboratories more in degree than in kind; that is, there is a comparatively higher degree of emphasis on skill building and comparatively less emphasis on awareness of feelings about oneself and others. There also is a comparatively higher degree of structure within the design and a liberal use of simulation activities. For the purpose of brevity, in this discussion we will refer to this type of training as executive development, but the content of this section generally will hold true for both management- and leadership-development programs.

Many skills are learned during an executive-development training event; they include listening, expressing, responding, participating, collaborating, facilitating, observing, intervening, reporting, conceptualizing, problem solving, decision making, planning, negotiating, collaborating, conflict management, and team building. We will discuss the ones that are listed first to provide examples, but we will not attempt to provide a subjective ranking of their importance within the training program.

Listening is a basic communication skill and it is reinforced throughout the training experience by means of structured activities and through the process of paraphrasing within small-group meetings. Expressing one's thoughts and feelings is practiced through nonverbal exercises, process-reporting exercises, intensive group meetings, and so on. Responding to the communication of others is the third basic communication skill that is reinforced. The intent here is for people to develop a heightened awareness of and sensitivity to the persons to whom they are responding so that they are able to communicate within a system that has meaning to others.

Leaders need to know how to be followers because following is a part of leading. Participating in group activities in which the "leader" is simply one of a group of people working shoulder-to-shoulder is an important skill and should be practiced during the training session. In developing skill in collaborating, participants are encouraged to learn how to use conflict functionally and to avoid conflict-reducing techniques (such as "horse trading") in order to determine the best judgement of the group in solving problems. Leaders need to develop the ability to facilitate other people's growth by encouraging them to take responsibility for the task that faces the group. Some skill building is needed in defining management/leadership as the facilitation or sharing of responsibility.

When observing, leaders need to be able to see the complexity of intra-individual, interindividual, intragroup, and intergroup phenomena, so some skill development should be planned within the program to help leaders to learn about the behavioral manifestations of interpersonal dynamics. Closely related to observing is skill in using what one sees to help a group to improve its own internal functioning by learning about its ongoing process. Leaders need to develop the consultation skill of process intervention. In addition, they need skills in reporting or summarizing large batches of group content in order to provide succinct accounts of what has been decided.

Conceptualizing is perhaps the most complex of executive skills. This involves looking at human interaction from a theoretical point of view. Conceptual models can be incorporated into executive-development training in a way that allows the participants to develop their own theories of management or leadership.

The following sequence is, we believe, an organic, logical, and effective flow of activities that need to take place in executive-development workshops. Again, this sequence is proposed as relevant whether the training takes place over a weekend or during a semester-long course.

Personal Growth

1. *Getting Acquainted.* The major need at the beginning of an event is for the par-

Executive Development

1. *Getting Acquainted.* Here the basic need is to infuse a note of psychological safety

ticipants to establish some familiarity with one another, so that the initial caution with which people interact can be eased. The unfreezing process begins in the initial stages of the event. Numerous getting-acquainted designs are available in the HRD literature and as structured experiences in the University Associates *Annual* and *Handbook* series.

2. *Closing Expectation Gaps.* It is important that the goals of the experience be made explicit and that they be correlated with the goals of the participants. It is equally important that participants and facilitators have a clear understanding of what each expects of the other. The most difficult training situation we know of exists when participants expect one kind of experience and staff members expect something else. Under this condition there needs to be immediate negotiation and clarification of assumptions.

3. *Legitimizing Risk Taking.* Early in the training experience, it is significant for participants to test their willingness to know and to be known by other people, to express their feelings, to explore

into the proceedings by familiarizing participants with one another and with staff members on a personal level. The effort is to create a climate in which people can have easy access to one another. It is important in the beginning of such an experience for people to be able to establish their credentials. Often participants feel a strong need to impress people with who and what they are.

2. *Closing Expectation Gaps.* In an executive-development workshop, as in a personal-growth training event, it is important that the goals of the experience be made explicit and correlated with the goals of participants. It is equally important that participants and staff members have a clear understanding of what each expects of the other. If the facilitator determines that there is a wide expectation gap, he or she must immediately negotiate to close it.

3. *Roles and Shared Leadership.* The concept of roles and functions of different group members and the notion of dynamic, shared leadership should be introduced. This sets the tone for using theoretical

how other people are reacting to them, and to attempt new ways of behaving in relation to other people. At this point it is important that risk taking be legitimized and reinforced as a norm in the training setting.

4. *Learning About Feedback*. Soon after the beginning of the personal growth event, it is useful to provide some instruction about the feedback process so that effective sharing can be heightened in the intensive, small-group sessions and in the free time between formally planned sessions. (See the "Guidelines for Giving and Receiving Feedback," Appendix 3 in *Using Role Plays in Human Resource Development,* the third book in the UA Training Technologies series.) Lecturettes, structured experiences, instruments, role plays, and trainer interventions can help to provide an atmosphere in which feedback becomes expected and experienced freely. These methods also can be used to introduce some conceptual models to guide participants in the sharing of information about one another.

5. *Developing an Awareness of Process*. After the intensive small group in a personal

material in an experiential format to focus on oneself as leader in relation to other people.

4. *Learning About Feedback*. Soon after the beginning of the training experience, it is useful to provide instruction in the feedback process so that effective sharing can be increased. Lecturettes, structured activities, instruments, and trainer interventions can help to provide an atmosphere in which feedback becomes expected and experienced freely.

5. *Developing an Awareness of Process*. After the executive-development training

growth event has had a brief history, it often is highly useful to begin to explore the dynamic processes that are emerging in the development of the group. This may be done through a fishbowl procedure or a variety of other designs previously discussed. The group can grow more rapidly if it stops occasionally in the interaction among members to process the patterns that are beginning to emerge in its development.

6. *Integrating Conceptual Models.* Transfer of learnings is more likely to be achieved if the participants receive assistance in integrating the behavioral and affective data of the experience by looking at some theoretical models of personal and group development. This can done through the use of instruments, lecturettes, demonstrations, and so on.

7. *Experimenting with Self-Expression.* Growth in awareness of self and others can be heightened through the use of expressive techniques such as nonverbal exercises and guided imagery. Toward the middle of the personal growth experience, often it is useful to build into the design some opportunity for people to

group has had a brief history, it is highly useful to begin to explore the dynamic processes emerging in the group. This may be done through a fishbowl procedure or a variety of other designs, many of which are discussed in this book. The group can develop effectively if it stops occasionally in the interaction among members to process the kinds of leadership and roles that are beginning to emerge.

6. *Competition Task.* Early in an executive-development event, it is a good idea to introduce an activity that is likely to result in participants' exploring the functional and dysfunctional effects of interpersonal competition. Sometimes a competitive atmosphere is established deliberately, such as in an intergroup model-building activity, or it may arise spontaneously in a relatively unstructured task experience.

7. *Collaboration Task.* It is useful to follow a competitive experience with an activity in which people are expected to attempt deliberately to collaborate with other people on a task. The aim is to demonstrate that collaboration is possible and desirable, even within a culture that rewards competitive spirit.

"stretch" their personal development through the use of symbolic self-expression.

8. *Planning Back-Home Applications.* Ideally, plans for back-home application begin to develop from the beginning of the training event. For example, an early experience that often is useful is a goal-setting activity, with reassessment in the middle and at the end of the event. Often we use role playing, contracting, and helping pairs for applying the learnings from the experience to particular back-home situations. Toward the end of the experience, considerable effort should be made toward getting participants to accept responsibility for making definite plans for changes that they want to institute after the training experience is over. These plans need to be evaluated in the light of criteria for application, and this evaluation often is best done in collaboration with one or two other individuals with whom the participant feels comfortable.

8. *Consensus Task.* Closely related to the collaboration task is consensus seeking. Many structured experiences can be chosen that involve a number of people in arriving at collective judgments that are superior to individual judgments. This kind of experience attempts to illustrate the concept of synergy.

9. *Assisting Re-Entry.* Closure activities in a personal growth experience should enable the participants to move back into their ordinary environments with a minimal amount of difficulty. Activities

9. *Planning Back-Home Applications.* Toward the end of the training experience it is important for the participants to begin making definite plans for particular behaviors that they want to experiment with

that emphasize feeling and cause participants to be "high" can result in dysfunctional re-entry into their immediate back-home situations. It is important to assist participants in exploring the observation that they are full of consciousness of themselves. At this point they are far more sensitive to their feelings and are more willing to be involved with people in open, trusting ways than are their "real-life" associates who have not just spent a considerable amount of time in a personal growth laboratory.

This general sequence does not imply a rigid structure. It simply is an attempt to highlight the needs of participants to develp an ability to talk with one another, to learn how to make sense out of the interaction that is occurring, and to heighten the development of ways in which they can use the experience in their everyday lives.

and/or change in their back-home management or leadership situations. It sometimes is useful to have participants write letters to themselves about what they are going to attempt to change, based on both cognitive material and their own experiences during the training.

In addition to a sequence of activities fostering skill building and the development of a set of concepts about management or leadership, some material is thematic throughout an executive-development training design. Three concepts should be stressed during the event itself: process awareness, criteria of effective feedback, and theories of management/leadership. The design of the executive-development workshop in general, then, consists of encouraging participants to experiment with leadership phenomena, involving them in a series of activities to explore leadership from the point of view of looking at themselves in roles, exploring group effects and the dynamics of competition and collaboration, and planning the transfer of learning to their management or leadership situations back home.

7

Professional Development in Design

Building a Repertoire

A number of steps can be taken to improve one's ability to design training experiences. A first step in developing such skill is to build a repertoire of materials that can be used in design work. The facilitator can become familiar with structured experiences and instruments available for use in training and can master an array of lecture materials that he or she can call on at a moment's notice to explain particular phenomena in the training setting. The "References and Bibliography" section at the end of this book provides an abundance of materials to aid the facilitator in this regard.

Co-Facilitating

A second step in improving one's ability to design training is to be active in seeking opportunities to work with a variety of other facilitators. This has a number of important advantages. One has the opportunity to observe what actually happens in the training setting and how things are handled by other facilitators. One can receive concentrated, highly specific feedback on one's style as a facilitator, can improve one's ability to diagnose participants' needs, and can spend staff time critiquing the design and debriefing training sessions after they are completed. This, we believe, is the best professional-development strategy currently available. There is no substitute for experience with other qualified professionals, working in a training setting with actual participants.

Varying Clients

A third step is to seek out opportunities to work with various client groups. This requires that the facilitator be flexible in design and avoid developing design packages that may be irrelevant to the learning needs of particular clients. There are obvious ethical restrictions on the facilitator in seeking out clients. Human-interaction training generally is considered to be a professional-level activity; therefore, professional ethics require that facilitators not over-represent their qualifications. Within ethical restrictions, however, one can grow professionally by generating experience in working with a variety of participants.

Studying Designs

Another activity that can result in professional development in designing training experiences is to study other facilitators' designs. This is a somewhat controversial subject in that, within the field of HRD, there is a tendency for facilitators to be closed and possessive about the designs they have developed. It is not uncommon for facilitators to conclude that they have developed a program that is highly salable, and one often encounters reluctance to share designs with other professionals. At some point, what happens is the systematic violation of a norm that we try to sell to clients: to be open and collaborative. University Associates conducted a life-planning workshop some time ago in which over half the participants attended primarily to learn how to conduct the program themselves. We renamed the event the "rip-off lab" and had a good laugh about it. What was significant about the experience was the fact that before the workshop began, the participants' hidden agenda was a taboo topic. We made it an open subject and legitimized it so that people would not feel the need to conceal their motives from the training staff.

In studying other facilitators' designs, however, it is important to remember that many designs are copyrighted and that studying a design to learn what works or what is unique is different from taking somebody else's design *in toto* and using it out of context.

Others' designs almost always are, in some aspect, irrelevant to the particular needs of another client system. Learning what works, how to create, and how to adapt should be the objective.

Attending Workshops

A fifth step that facilitators can take is to attend professional-development workshops. Many learning experiences are available for the human resource development professional that afford opportunities to obtain supervised practice in the design of training laboratories. Various training organizations, such as the National Training Laboratories and University Associates, offer such professional-development programs.

Attending Labs as a Participant

Finally, it is very useful for the facilitator to attend training events occasionally as a participant rather than as a staff member. The human element is the critical point in effective facilitation. The most significant ethical boundary impinging on HRD professionals is the need to remain healthy: not to deceive themselves about who they are, what they are up to, where they are going, and so on. Experiencing training as a participant means living by the same kind of values that we are attempting to teach other people and continuing to develop our ability to provide experiences that offer meaningful human contact with other people. The major need in staff development is to integrate one's personal and professional development. Personal growth is necessary but not sufficient; even though the facilitator may be a highly effective person, he or she still needs the technology of laboratory education in order to be effective in fostering the development of other people.

Practicing with Others

The following are a dozen suggestions for the members of planning teams who want to enhance their design skills.

1. Agree on the general goals of the session you are planning (and the topical area that participants will explore during your practice session).
2. Develop a few ideas privately (individually).
3. Share your individual ideas and augment them spontaneously.
4. Evaluate ideas privately (individually).
5. Share your evaluations and identify areas of agreement.
6. By consensus, select the most salient idea. (Remember that the objective of this practice session is to provide you with an opportunity to learn about design from having designed and implemented a short training model, not to create a perfect design.)
7. Develop a design that will allow your participants to:
   - *Experience* (an activity that generates useful data);
   - *Reflect* on what was experienced (share reactions and observations; compare reactions and dynamics and clarify learnings; and develop principles, hypotheses, and hunches about the relevance of their learning to outside issues); and
   - *Apply* (plan new behaviors in realistic situations based on the learning that has emerged).
8. Try out your design within the team, if possible.
9. Solicit reactions to the design from an external consultant, if possible.
10. Conduct the design with workshop participants, soliciting detailed criticisms.
11. Reconvene with your planning group. Review the results of your session. Debrief team functioning and learnings gained from having worked as a member of the team on this design.
12. Modify the design and invent variations, if possible.

Pilot Programs

As indicated above, a test run of a design module or full design can be a very worthwhile endeavor if the situation warrants it. For example, such a situation might exist if you do not have a lot of experience in designing training modules, if you want to use something that may generate a lot of affect or be tricky in some way, if you are just not sure about the design, or if the training will be conducted for a large number of people and you want to be sure that they do not perceive it as a waste of money. Running a pilot program also can be a way of sending a message that you work carefully, but this can backfire if you are perceived as being overcautious or inexperienced. As the preceding list indicates, a trial run enables you to obtain specialized feedback for evaluation.

The best group for a pilot program is a receptive audience of decision influencers—not the type of people who have a "show me" attitude but those who can provide constructive and useful feedback and advice.

8

Selecting Training Sites

The selection of an appropriate physical setting for a training workshop is a critical variable in the learning process. Although the "perfect" place does not exist, it is important that the advantages and disadvantages of a site be weighed carefully against the goals of each event to maximize the participants' learning potential.

Location and Setting

Training that takes participants away from their place of work eliminates the distractions of their daily routines and the interference of their colleagues. This contributes positively to the investment and involvement that participants have in the training event. When workshops last more than one day, it is ideal to have people sleep and eat at the site. Informal interaction among participants is increased and contributes to their learning, much of which occurs outside the regular workshop.

Ease of transportation and proximity to public carriers (e.g., airports) are important considerations for a public workshop. Getting to and from the training site can become a major dissatisfier if directions are not clear, costs are too high, or travel time is too long. A useful rule of thumb is to hold public events within forty-five minutes of a major airport and near major cities. Going into a major city is a plus for many participants.

The basic considerations for training settings are privacy, attractive grounds and buildings, a humanistic staff, moderate costs, and limited distractions. We strongly prefer "retreat" settings, if possible. Both religious and nonreligious locations where the staff is accustomed to offering service and direct support to conferences and workshops are satisfactory sites. Many colleges and universities also have excellent facilities available, especially in the summer months. There also are several professionally run conference centers located in various parts of the United States, but they tend to be more expensive than nonprofit locations.

Many facilitators choose motels and hotels as training sites, but most motels and hotels do not meet the basic considerations. Although hotels often cater to conferences, because the house staff usually is not well trained to meet the unique needs of a workshop design and the meeting rooms often are either too sterile or too ornate, much of the trainer's energy may be spent in coordinating details and solving problems. However, these difficulties can be minimized by careful shopping, close coordination with the contact persons, and a visit to the location in advance.

The following are useful resources for finding and selecting workshop sites:

- *Official Meeting Facilities Guide.* Published semiannually by the Business Publications Division of Murdoch Magazines, a division of News America Publishing, Incorporated, in Secaucus, New Jersey.

- *Hotel & Motel Red Book: The Official American Hotel & Motel Association Lodging Directory for the Business Traveler.* Published annually by PacTel Publishing, 590 Ygnacio Valley Road, Suite 300, Walnut Creek, California 94596.

- *OAG* (Official Airline Guide). Published every other month by Official Airline Guides, Inc., 2000 Clearwater Drive, Oak Brook, Illinois 60521.

Country clubs are another type of site to consider. During their off-seasons, the rates are more moderate than those of hotels, and clubs often possess many of the physical and service advantages offered by retreat houses. Another plus is that, as with colleges and universities, there usually are excellent recreational facilities available. Physical activities during breaks in the schedule can add needed variety to a workshop. If a beautiful site with excellent recreational facilities is selected, time should be planned to allow participants to use those facilities.

Room and Board Arrangements

A variety of room and board arrangements can be negotiated with sites, but there are two basic options: (a) a daily rate for room, meals, and refreshments and (b) a sleeping rate only, which allows participants to take responsibility for their own meals wherever they choose. These two options often can be combined in various degrees.

The first option is advantageous for some participants but it can be a problem for those with special dietary needs. The second option provides for individual preferences on the part of participants but may fail to foster a climate of community.

The choice of options should be based directly on the goals of the event. If team building is the goal, for example, the prearranged community meal arrangement is the best choice. If individual learning is the goal, allowing participants to be responsible for their own meals is an appropriate and simpler choice. The facilitator should be aware of these factors in considering, for example, the choice of a retreat setting where only prearranged meals are available or a hotel in a city known for good restaurants.

Meals that provide the greatest variety for the least cost are a basic concern when selecting a training site. Cafeteria or buffet service is preferable to served meals because of the time and menu flexibility. Most retreat centers, colleges, universities, and conference centers offer this type of meal plan as a package with the room rate. However, it is important to check on the availability of vegetarian plates, diet drinks, etc.

Whether to include the cost of arranged meals in the workshop fee when using hotels and motels is always a question. Because of the problems of forty-eight-hour guarantees, costly menu items, and the relative inflexibility of serving time and range of choices, we often decide to have participants at our workshops eat in the coffee shop or at nearby restaurants. Such a decision does diminish the group's sense of community, but it is usually easier for the participants. However, one major advantage to having the hotel serve lunches and/or dinners is that the meeting room (which often exceeds $100 a day) is usually free.

Even if meals are not included in the training package, it is a good idea to have coffee and tea available in the meeting room. The trainer can arrange for an informal setup that is checked by the house staff prior to the start of each session. There usually is an extra charge for this service, but many places include it in the room rate. Soft drinks may be fairly expensive, but they should be included when the workshop is being held in a warm climate. Refreshment costs, like many other necessary incidentals during a training event, can mount rapidly and become a major expense if not carefully monitored.

It is useful to arrange an after-hours social event with beer, wine, and soft drinks to help promote informal interaction and learning. (Many trainers schedule only 8 a.m. to 5 p.m. days, but we think that too many free nights detract from the importance of the workshop; during week-long events, however, a night off in the middle of the event is a good idea.) It is important to check the alcohol policies of the training site; sometimes liquor is prohibited, or there may be a requirement that the site provide a bartender, usually at considerable cost. If a hotel is used, the trainer can rent a large suite for parties and ask that participants contribute to the refreshment fund.

If participants will be paying for their room and board separate from the tuition, it is convenient to negotiate a fixed daily rate that each person pays directly to the site. The "administrivia" of number of meals, single and double rooms, extra charges, etc., can be time consuming if assumed by the facilitator. If such a direct arrangement is not possible, one staff person can be designated to handle all the details with the site and to collect money and organize arrangements with the participants. The primary goal is to minimize problems and distractions from the participants' point of view.

Psychological Setting

Outcomes for those involved in a training event can be dramatically impacted by the psychological setting of the site. If the site has rigid rules and people who disapprove strongly of any behavior that deviates from the conservative norm (such as crying or touching), the trainer obviously should not choose that site for conducting a personal-growth lab. Trainers are strongly advised to consider the goals and content of the training event and to select a site that will contribute to the achievement of those goals.

Privacy

The degree of privacy required in a training site varies with the purpose of the training. If the event has a personal-growth focus, it is more important to provide a high degree of privacy for participants in the training room and the living accommodations. Participants are more likely to experiment with new behavior of a very personal nature in a setting that is safe from prying or judgmental eyes. If the event is less personal in its orientation and interaction is less intense, the requirement for privacy is lessened. However, some level of privacy that precludes strangers from wandering into meeting rooms and encourages participants to interact with one another during and between sessions is advisable in any training event. In organization development meetings, for example, much of the material discussed may be proprietary and confidential and require a degree of privacy.

A very important variable in privacy concerns the other groups using the site and the degree of probability that the groups will intermingle or share facilities and create dysfunctional competition and annoyances, draining energy away from the purpose of the event.

Comfort

The color, lighting, condition, and general aesthetic quality of meeting and living areas can have a dramatic effect on the learning that takes place. If the areas are drab or uncomfortable, a great deal of energy may be displaced into complaining and negative projections. If the site is extravagantly decorated or contains obviously religious art, the decoration may distract from the training content. A relatively neutral but pleasant environment seems to work best. It is wise to select a site with adequate light that is adjustable to the needs of the event and a color scheme such as pale green, off-white, or beige. Too many large windows also can be a distraction.

In general, the site should be of an aesthetic quality similar to that with which most participants are familiar.

Size of Meeting Rooms

No one likes to be crammed into a cubicle in which body heat alone can raise the temperature fifteen degrees in one hour. Nor do most people enjoy the feeling of a ten-person group lost in an auditorium designed to seat five hundred. Experience indicates that twenty-five square feet per person attending the event is a good rule of thumb. The shape of the room also is crucial. It should be square rather than long and narrow. This criterion is one of the most difficult to meet at many sites; the trainer often may be forced to compromise to some degree. The larger the number of participants, of course, the bigger the problem. Ceiling height does not seem to have a great deal of effect as long as it is not less than eight feet (if it is lower than this, many people tend to feel smothered).

If more or fewer participants than expected appear, the trainer should look into the possibility of obtaining a different meeting room.

Normal Usage of Site

Meeting sites usually are designed with some specific purpose in mind. Older sites often were constructed for classroom arrangements, which may or may not prove adequate for a training event. Many new sites, however, are designed to accommodate laboratory learning. The purpose for which the site is used most often will give the trainer some indication of the psychological climate. If it is a country club or resort, it may be more conducive to recreation than learning. Heavy drinking may be a norm, detracting from the purpose of the event. If it is a religious retreat site, there may be very strong norms that (although peripheral to the operation of the site) may cause considerable consternation and goal diffusion for many participants. Such issues as "quiet hours," dress codes, normal age range, and the level of the staff's psychological ownership of the site may pose serious problems for or contribute materially to the success of the event. An "uptight" site manager may turn an otherwise successful event into a psychological disaster for trainers and participants alike. Whether it seems plausible or not, the behavior of a busperson assigned to the meeting area can have a great deal of influence on the participants' learning. (The incentive of a good tip contingent on the achievement of very specific behaviors can ameliorate a problem in this area better than a complaint to the management.)

Philosophy of Site Management

It is crucial to the success of an event that the training objectives and procedures do not violate the philosophy or behavioral norms of the site staff. For example, if egg throwing is part of the workshop design, the trainer had better have a very direct conversation with the site management *before* signing a contract. On the other hand, if the event is designed for senior executives, bishops, or senior citizens, the trainer would do well to look for a site not known for its radical ideas and norms. A humanistic leadership workshop is likely to do better at a site that is managed humanistically than at a site that is rigidly controlled.

Whenever possible, it is a good idea for trainers to visit a potential site, prior to contracting for its use, in order to experience its psychological climate. Many commercial sites will provide trainers with a complimentary stay, and it is advisable to take advantage of the offer if at all possible. It may make a great deal of difference in the final decision. If trainers cannot visit the site, they should talk with someone who has been there. In any case, they should ask the site to provide references from other users.

Negotiating and Contracting

The best advice in this category is to know exactly what the selection criteria are for a particular event and then shop around for the best match. The trainer should remember that in most cases it is a buyer's market. It is not necessary to grab the offer unless everything, including the price, is perfect. Shrewd shopping and hard bargaining can substantially reduce costs.

Some things to consider in negotiating:

1. *Cost of refreshments.* Are they priced per gallon or per person? An arrangement that allows payment only for what actually is used is almost always best.

2. *Meeting room rates.* It is standard practice for these rates to be prorated, based on the number of sleeping rooms and/or meals scheduled. If over twenty sleeping rooms are used, the meeting room should be free.

3. *Payment terms.* Are all fees payable on departure, or are thirty-, sixty-, or ninety-day terms available?

4. *Advance deposit.* Some sites require this; for a public event, such a requirement could well be a disqualifier.

5. *Specific contact.* It is very important to be sure that one person from the site management who is going to be on site throughout the duration of the event is specified by name. If at all possible, the trainer should talk with this representative in advance to discuss the concerns and desires of the workshop. It is necessary to listen carefully and be sure that there is a clear mutual understanding of all requirements. When the newsprint supply runs out or the air conditioning goes off, this person is the one to call. Without such a contact, the division of labor at many sites among housekeeping, catering, sales, room reservations, and maintenance can be very trying to deal with.

6. *Advance reservations.* Perhaps most important is to make reservations as far in advance as possible so that the features of the site can be utilized to best advantage.

If the trainer conducts similar events frequently, it may be useful to prepare a "request for bid" document that outlines all requirements, schedules, etc., in detail, leaving blank spaces for the site management to fill in with exact prices. This will help to ensure that needs and desires are met and that there are no surprises on the final bill. This document should be submitted to the site far in advance of the event, and the site management should know that bids from other sites also are being requested.

Another helpful item for the use of the facilitator is a check list for site selection (see the sample that follows). By checking off each item as it is completed or dealt with, the facilitator can keep track of the state of the negotiations with the site.

There is a wide variety of concerns and options relating to choosing a training site, and tradeoffs in administering a particular workshop at a particular site always exist. Thoughtful choices, attention to details, and hard negotiation will help to make the site a positive contribution to the success of a workshop.

A Sample Check List for Site Selection

Instructions: Use one copy of this check list for each site being considered. In discussing the site with sales personnel, be sure to cover each item, check it off, and make any pertinent notes. A consideration of all the items on this check list will provide a sound basis for contracting. Be sure to add any special requirements that you have.

Site Being Considered: _____

Event: _____

Goals of the Training: _____

Participants: _____

Staff: _____

Points to Consider:

_____ Sleep at site

_____ Type and cost of sleeping rooms

_____ Price of food

_____ Prearranged meals or individual responsibility

_____ Cafeteria or waited tables

_____ Special dietary requirements

_____ Limited distractions

_____ Humanistic and competent staff

_____ Appropriateness of *usual* use of site

_____ Quiet hours

_____ Size of meeting room

_____ Multiple room requirement

_____ Cost of meeting room(s)

_____ Complimentary sleeping rooms for staff

_____ Privacy

_____ Type of furniture in meeting rooms

_____ Audiovisual equipment available

_____ Attractiveness and quality of decor in meeting rooms

_____ Water, tea, and soft drinks available during sessions

_____ Dress codes

_____ Usual age group of people using the site

_____ Presence of other groups

_____ Reservation as far in advance as possible

_____ Cost of refreshments

_____ Ease of transportation and proximity to public carriers

_____ Policies regarding alcohol and smoking

Advance deposit required? _____ by _____

Credit terms _____

Precontracting visit to site _____

Name of one person on site staff to coordinate all needs before, during,

and after event _____

References and Bibliography

Banet, A.G. (1974). Therapeutic intervention and the perception of process. In J.W. Pfeiffer & J.E. Jones (Eds.), *The 1974 annual handbook for group facilitators*. San Diego, CA: University Associates.

Benne, K.D., Bradford, L.P., Gibb, J.R., & Lippitt, R.O. (Eds). (1975). *The laboratory method of changing and learning: Theory and applications*. Palo Alto, CA: Science and Behavior Books.

Boone, T.A. (1975). Therapy or personal growth? In J.E. Jones & J.W. Pfeiffer (Eds.), *The 1975 annual handbook for group facilitators*. San Diego, CA: University Associates.

Boone, T.A., & Reid, R.A. (1978). Selecting workshop sites. In J.W. Pfeiffer & J.E. Jones (Eds.), *The 1978 annual handbook for group facilitators*. San Diego, CA: University Associates.

Bouchard, T.J. (1976). Field research methods: Interviewing, questionnaires, participant observation, systematic observation, unobtrusive measures. In M.D. Dunnette (Ed.), *Handbook of industrial and organizational psychology*. Chicago: Rand McNally.

Bradford, L.P., Gibb, J.R., & Benne, K.D. (Eds.). (1964). *T-group theory and laboratory method*. New York: John Wiley.

Bunker, B.B., Nochajski, T., McGillicuddy, N., & Bennett, D. (1987). Designing and running training events: Rules of thumb for trainers. In W.B. Reddy & C.C. Henderson, Jr., (Eds.), *Training theory and practice*. Arlington, VA: NTL Institute for Applied Behavioral Science/San Diego, CA: University Associates.

Bunning, R.L. (1979). The Delphi technique: A projection tool for serious inquiry. In J.E. Jones & J.W. Pfeiffer (Eds.), *The 1979 annual handbook for group facilitators*. San Diego, CA: University Associates.

Carnevale, A.P. (1986). The learning enterprise. *Training and Development Journal, 40,* 18-26.

Cohen, A.M., & Smith, R.D. (1976). *The critical incident in growth groups: Theory and technique*. San Diego, CA: University Associates.

Cooke, P., & Bates, R.R. (1989). Evaluation: Issues first, methodology second. In J.W. Pfeiffer (Ed.), *The 1989 annual: developing human resources*. San Diego, CA: University Associates.

Cooper, C.L., & Harrison, K. (1976). Designing and facilitating experiential group activities: Variables and issues. In J.W. Pfeiffer & J.E. Jones (Eds.), *The 1976 annual handbook for group facilitators*. San Diego, CA: University Associates.

Custer, G.E. (1986). *Planning, packaging, and presenting training: A guide for subject-matter experts*. San Diego, CA: University Associates.

Davis, L.N. (1974). *Planning, conducting, and evaluating workshops*. San Diego, CA: Learning Concepts/University Associates.

Delbecq, A.L., Van de Ven, A.H., & Gustafson, D.H. (1975). *Group techniques for program planning*. Glenview, IL: Scott, Foresman.

Egan, G. (1972). Contracts in encounter groups. In J.W. Pfeiffer & J.E. Jones (Eds.), *The 1972 annual handbook for group facilitators*. San Diego, CA: University Associates.

Feldman, D.C. (1988). Designing more effective orientation programs. In J.W. Pfeiffer (Ed.), *The 1988 annual: Developing human resources*. San Diego, CA: University Associates.

Festinger, L. (1957). *A theory of cognitive dissonance*. Palo Alto, CA: Stanford University Press.

Festinger, L. (1964). *Conflict, decision, and dissonance*. Palo Alto, CA: Stanford University Press.

Ford, D.L., Jr. (1975). Nominal group technique: An applied group problem-solving activity. In J.E. Jones & J.W. Pfeiffer (Eds.), *The 1975 annual handbook for group facilitators*. San Diego, CA: University Associates.

Freedman, A.M. (1978). Types of process interventions. In J.W. Pfeiffer & J.E. Jones (Eds.), *The 1978 annual handbook for group facilitators*. San Diego, CA: University Associates.

Goad, T.W. (1982). *Delivering effective training*. San Diego, CA: University Associates.

Hanson, P.G. (1981). *Learning through groups: A trainer's basic guide*. San Diego, CA: University Associates.

Jones, J.E. (1972). Types of growth groups. In J.W. Pfeiffer & J.E. Jones (Eds.), *The 1972 annual handbook for group facilitators*. San Diego, CA: University Associates.

Jones, J.E. (1973). The sensing interview. In J.E. Jones & J.W. Pfeiffer (Eds.), *The 1973 annual handbook for group facilitators.* San Diego, CA: University Associates.

Karp, H.B. (1985). The use of the training contract. In L.D. Goodstein & J.W. Pfeiffer (Eds.), *The 1985 annual: Developing human resources.* San Diego, CA: University Associates.

Kay, C.R., Peyton, S.K., & Pike, R. (1987). Diagnosing the training situation: Matching instructional techniques with learning outcomes and environment. In J.W. Pfeiffer (Ed.), *The 1987 annual: Developing human resources.* San Diego, CA: University Associates.

Knowles, M. (1972). *The modern practice of adult education.* Chicago: Association Press/Follett.

Knowles, M. (1975.) *Self-directed learning.* Chicago: Association Press/Follett.

Knowles, M. (1978). *The adult learner: A neglected species* (2nd ed.). Houston, TX: Gulf.

Lewin, K. (1947). Frontiers in group dynamics: I. Concept, method, and reality in social sciences: Social equilibria and social change. *Human Relations, 1*(1), 5-41.

Mayo, C.D., & DuBois, P.H. (1987). *The complete book of training: Theory, principles, and techniques.* San Diego, CA: University Associates.

Middleman, R.R., & Goldberg, G. (1972). The concept of structure in experiential learning. In J.W. Pfeiffer & J.E. Jones (Eds.), *The 1972 annual handbook for group facilitators.* San Diego, CA: University Associates.

Mill, C.R. (1980). *Activities for trainers: 50 useful designs.* San Diego, CA: University Associates.

Miller, S., Nunnally, E.W., & Wackman, D.B. (1976). The awareness wheel. In J.E. Jones & J.W. Pfeiffer (Eds.), *The 1976 annual handbook for group facilitators.* San Diego, CA: University Associates.

Nadler, D.A. (1977). *Feedback and organization development: Using data-based methods.* Reading, MA: Addison-Wesley.

Palmer, A.B. (1981). Learning cycles: Models of behavioral change. In J.E. Jones & J.W. Pfeiffer (Eds.), *The 1981 annual handbook for group facilitators.* San Diego, CA: University Associates.

Pfeiffer, J.W. (Ed.). (1983, 1985). *A handbook of structured experiences for human relations training* (Vols. IX and X). San Diego, CA: University Associates.

Pfeiffer, J.W. (Ed.). (1987-1989). *The annual: Developing human resources.* San Diego, CA: University Associates.

Pfeiffer, J.W., & Goodstein, L.D. (Eds.). (1982, 1983). *The annual for facilitators, trainers, and consultants.* San Diego, CA: University Associates.

Pfeiffer, J.W., & Goodstein, L.D. (Eds.). (1984-1986). *The annual: Developing human resources.* San Diego, CA: University Associates.

Pfeiffer, J.W., & Jones, J.E. (Eds.). (1969, 1970, 1971, 1973, 1974, 1975, 1977, 1979, 1981). *A handbook of structured experiences for human relations training* (Vols. I, II, III, IV, V, VI, VII, and VIII). San Diego, CA: University Associates.

Pfeiffer, J.W., & Jones, J.E. (Eds.). (1972-1981). *The annual handbook for group facilitators.* San Diego, CA: University Associates.

Pfeiffer, J.W., & Jones, J.E. (1974). Brainstorming: A problem-solving activity. In J.W. Pfeiffer & J.E. Jones (Eds.), *A handbook of structured experiences for human relations training* (Vol. III). San Diego, CA: University Associates.

Pfeiffer, J.W., & Jones, J.E. (1975). Co-facilitating. In J.E. Jones & J.W. Pfeiffer (Eds.), *The 1975 annual handbook for group facilitators.* San Diego, CA: University Associates.

Pfeiffer, J.W., & Jones, J.E. (1983). *Structured experience kit.* San Diego, CA: University Associates.

Pfeiffer, J.W., & Pfeiffer, J.A. (1975). A Gestalt primer. In J.E. Jones & J.W. Pfeiffer (Eds.), *The 1975 annual handbook for group facilitators.* San Diego, CA: University Associates.

Rao, T.V., & Pareek, U. (1980). Organizing and conducting microlabs for training. In J.W. Pfeiffer & J.E. Jones (Eds.), *The 1980 annual handbook for group facilitators.* San Diego, CA: University Associates.

Simpson, D.T. (1983). A model for training design: Selecting appropriate methods. In L.D. Goodstein & J.W. Pfeiffer (Eds.), *The 1983 annual for facilitators, trainers, and consultants.* San Diego, CA: University Associates.

Spier, M.S. (1973). Kurt Lewin's "force field analysis." In J.E. Jones & J.W. Pfeiffer (Eds.), *The 1973 annual handbook for group facilitators.* San Diego, CA: University Associates.

Swanson, R.A., & Geroy, G.D. (1987). Forecasting the economic benefits of training. In J.W. Pfeiffer (Ed.), *The 1987 annual: Developing human resources.* San Diego, CA: University Associates.

Thomas, J. (1984). Needs assessment: Avoiding the "hammer" approach. In J.W. Pfeiffer & L.D. Goodstein (Eds.), *The 1984 annual: Developing human resources.* San Diego, CA: University Associates.

Thomas, J.G., & Sireno, P.J. (1980). Assessing management competency needs. *Training and Development Journal, 34*(9), 47-51.

Tough, A. (1979). *The adult's learning projects* (2nd ed.). San Diego, CA: Learning Concepts.

Warshauer, S. (1988). *Inside training & development: Creating effective programs.* San Diego, CA: University Associates.